FOLLOWING CREATION

Smyth & Helwys Publishing, Inc.
6316 Peake Road
Macon, Georgia 31210-3960
1-800-747-3016
©2024 by Gregory Funderburk
All rights reserved.

Library of Congress Cataloging-in-Publication Data

Names: Funderburk, Gregory, 1965- author.
Title: Following creation : a more sacred path from Monday to Sunday / by Gregory Funderburk.
Description: First. | Macon : Smyth & Helwys, 2023. | Includes bibliographical references.
Identifiers: LCCN 2023049194 | ISBN 9781641734738 (alk. paper)
Subjects: LCSH: Christian life. | Creation--Biblical teaching.
Classification: LCC BV4501.3 .F856 2023 | DDC 248.4--dc23/eng/20231207
LC record available at lccn.loc.gov/2023049194

Disclaimer of Liability: With respect to statements of opinion or fact available in this work of nonfiction, Smyth & Helwys Publishing Inc. nor any of its employees, makes any warranty, express or implied, or assumes any legal liability or responsibility for the accuracy or completeness of any information disclosed, or represents that its use would not infringe privately-owned rights.

Advance Praise for *Following Creation*

Greg Funderburk has a demonstrated gift for drawing captivating stories to an incisive point, like reversing a rainbow back into white light without losing any of the color. With *Following Creation*, the focused beam of his prose graciously challenges readers with each meditation. I am grateful he has shared his gift again.

—*Eric Black*
Executive Director, Publisher & Editor, Baptist Standard

If, in the dark nights of your soul or in the glory of Easter Sundays, you find yourself grasping for the hand of a traveling companion, boy, do we have the book for you. Greg Funderburk is witty and whimsical, while also bearing the scars of a live well-lived. While many daily devotionals offer a great deal of fluff and little into which one might sink their teeth, *Following Creation*, does just that. Rev. Funderburk offers us readers reflections worth chewing on. Bon appetit, friends!

—*Rev. Dr. Kevin Gardner-Sinclair*
Pastor of Broadway Baptist Church, Louisville, Kentucky

In *Following Creation: A More Sacred Path from Monday to Sunday*, Greg Funderburk employs both an impressive breadth of reading material and his ability to apply wisdom and truths from his reading to everyday life. He skillfully weaves insights into his personal life in a way that enlivens our understanding of God's Presence and activity. Truly, like Wordsworth, Greg "sees a world in a grain of sand and a heaven in a wild flower," noticing, observing, paying attention to the details of life and in books in such a way that he makes the reader wake up, as well. I love this book, and as a reader and a writer, I am inspired and encouraged by these daily readings.

—*Jeanie Miley*
Author of Fierce Love: Radical Measures for Desperate Times

I don't know when Greg's mind rests, but it's not when he writes. Drawing from a trove of stories and wisdom gleaned from his voracious reading, he shares encouraging, often inspiring, day-by-day paths of hope leading to transformative weekly worship.

—*James Randall O'Brien*
Former Provost, Baylor University
President Emeritus, Carson-Newman University
Author of Would Moses Throw a Chair?

Greg Funderburk is at it again, offering learned, limpid meditations regarding thoughtful, faithful Christ-following! Patterned after the account of creation recorded in Genesis 1, *Following Creation* is a collection of sixty substantive reflections that creatively and gently guide us to "number our days, not so much counting them as making them count. Deeply humane, consistently insightful, and frequently funny, I will keep this volume handy for daily devotional reading so that I might lead a more devoted life.

—*Todd D. Still, PhD*
Charles J. and Eleanor McLerran DeLancey Dean &
William M. Hinson Professor of Christian Scriptures
Baylor University, Truett Seminary

Greg Funderburk is a Renaissance figure in our midst. Greg has a marvelous ability to take a simple thought or single word, to plumb its depths, and to bring out both a profound idea and a practical suggestion for living faith-fully today. This book is an excellent gift—for yourself or for someone you love. You can read it in a sitting, but it is better taken in slowly, with plenty of time between readings to ponder and reflect allowing each day's word to find home in your heart.

—*Steve Wells, DMin*
Pastor, South Main Baptist Church, Houston, Texas

GREGORY FUNDERBURK

FOLLOWING
Creation

A MORE SACRED PATH
FROM MONDAY TO SUNDAY

Also by Gregory Funderburk

The Mourning Wave
A Novel of the Great Storm

Let It Be Said We've Borne It Well
Following God in the Time of Covid-19

Hurdles
An Authentic Pursuit of God in a Post-Pandemic World

*To my wife, Kelly,
graceful and beautiful—the best of souls.
Through whom the best of life has come.*

Acknowledgments

Each week over the last three years, I've written an essay for Houston's South Main Baptist Church and those connected with it. The essays are published online Monday mornings, emailed to our members, and disseminated through social media. I'm very thankful to South Main for affording me the opportunity to write and for the encouragement I receive from the church. Thank you to Susan Moore, Jan Barkley, and Suzann Herrmann for making all this happen each week and to Dr. Steve Wells, who helps each person on our staff find and lean into their gifts.

My wife, Kelly, is crucial to everything I write—both in terms of process and final product. With wisdom and sensitivity, she steers me away from bad ideas and affirms the good ones I stumble into, helping me to express the themes I take up with clarity. My deep gratitude is also extended to those at Smyth & Helwys who shepherded this book into being with great expertise and guidance. Thanks especially to Keith Gammons, Holly Bean, and Leslie Andres in this regard.

Contents

Introduction: Seven Days

Monday: Light

1. The Courage to Encourage	3
2. Mercy	7
3. Humility	11
4. Forbearance	15
5. A Lasting Good	19
6. Our Very Best	23
7. Empathy	27
8. A Renegade Good Will	31
9. Gratitude	35
10. A New Dawn	39

Tuesday: Order

11. Single-Tasking	45
12. Remove One	49
13. Two Lenses	53
14. Focus	57
15. The Law of the Gift	61
16. Agency	65
17. Legibility	69
18. The Line	73
19. Furthermore, I Propose . . .	77
20. It All Accumulates	81

Wednesday: Growth

21. School	87
22. The Dishes	91
23. The Till	95
24. Shaping Conscience	99
25. Trying Enough Cases	103
26. Healing	105
27. Botherations	109
28. Baggage	113
29. If the World Were Perfect . . .	117
30. Wisdom	121

Thursday: Awe

31. Do You Give the Horse Its Strength . . .	127
32. Ephemeral	131
33. Unreservedly	135
34. The Fullness of Reality	139
35. Don't Look a Gift Universe in the Mouth	143
36. The Holy Act of Noticing	147
37. Astonishing	151
38. Heaven and Earth Commingled	155
39. You're Doing a Good Job	159
40. If Ruth Could among Alien Corn . . .	163

Friday: Imagination

41. Saints and Poets	169
42. Jude and Revelation	173
43. Looking for the Scintilla	177
44. More	181
45. Observe	185
46. Please Remain Seated	189
47. Banking on Hope	193
48. A New Kind of New	197
49. I Wonder	201
50. Love Songs	205

Saturday: Community

51. Carry Each Other	211
52. Failures of Kindness	215
53. The Dances You've Already Had	219
54. Mistrust the Rush	223
55. Tribe	227
56. Getting Home	231
57. Eleanor Rigby	235
58. The Fire	239
59. The Effect of Your Being	243
60. I Wish I'd Known That about Him . . .	247

Epilogue: Sunday

Introduction

Seven Days

While you might want to read this book from the first chapter to last in the ordinary way, the premise of this book entertains the possibility that, embedded within the biblical creation narrative, God might be suggesting a particular discipleship practice we ought to pursue on Mondays in particular, then another one on Tuesdays, and yet another on Wednesdays, Thursdays, Fridays, and Saturdays, before worship and rest on Sundays.

As you see in the contents, the book is divided into days of the week with ten chapters in each. Consider reading the first chapter under the heading Monday on a Monday; then on Tuesday, read the first entry under Tuesday, then go on from there to each day of the week, turning back to the next Monday entry only when Monday comes back around again.

Reading the book in this way represents a way to truly follow creation. I hope if you do this, day after day, week after week, the practice will help you develop the habit of taking up in some measure the beautiful work God took up each day as referenced in the opening pages of Genesis.

God commands us to set aside a particular day—the Sabbath—to rest just as God did following the work of creation. It's interesting that God doesn't seem to give us any instructions to follow with respect to other weekdays. While we're certainly encouraged to pray every day, to follow high ethical standards, and to take up a host of religious disciplines and spiritual practices, there's no specific reference to a practice or even a thematic regimen to follow on the day after the Sabbath. Or the next day, or the next. The Bible does not say anything like here's something to do in the middle of each week, or here's a particular idea to focus on as the week winds down.

Or maybe there *are* such instructions. Not highly regulated. Not legalistic in nature. But perhaps they exist all the same. Maybe they're hiding in plain sight on the first page of the book God has given to us on how we ought to live.

If we want to commune with God more closely within the thrumming pulse of our work—weeks full of trials and challenges—we might take a deeper look into the same creation narrative that offers us the theme of rest on the holy Sabbath. We might track what God did throughout that first week and follow its path in our lives. Perhaps by emulating, at least metaphorically, God's activity on each day of that first week, we might better grasp what God is doing in the world now. We might also find a more sustainable rhythm for communion with the divine and further meaning in our lives each week as we follow along. That's the premise of this book.

In Genesis 1, we read that on the first day—the day we think of as Monday—God said, "Let there be light," and light appeared. What if this illuminating activity suggests a thematic routine we might follow as we start our own week? What if each Monday we took up this notion of deliberately casting a ray of light out into the world and participating in the work that light represents—offering hope, joy, understanding, brightness, optimism, and a cleansing presence to an often dark and shadowy world? This practice could connect us to God's purposes on the first day of the week.

We read that on the second day God separated the sky from the chaos of the sea. What if, just as God did, we used our Tuesdays to bring order to the existing chaos of our world? What if on the second day of our work week, we looked for places where things are disordered and tried to clean them up? We could focus on this task each Tuesday, joining with God in the sacred nature of the holy second day.

On the third day, God separated the land and sea and created the grass, plants, and all that grows in and on the earth. What if we took up the notion of growth on Wednesdays, examining our lives more closely for areas of good growth that we know God wants to nurture within us? In the middle of our week, we could join God in the work of cultivating what is good and growing.

On the fourth day, God made the sun, moon, and stars. What if each Thursday, we simply made time for awe? We might more likely encounter God if we placed ourselves amid God's awe-inspiring fourth day of creative work.

On the fifth day, God created the animals. What if we used our Fridays to exercise our imagination as God did in creating these incredible creatures with whom we share the world on land, in the air, and under the sea. This was God's fifth day of work. It could be ours too as we more closely connect with the divine near the end of a busy week. Fridays are for creating something beautiful.

On the sixth day, God created us. God made human beings. What if, just as God did, we intentionally aimed each Saturday to create community with our spouses, friends, partners, children, siblings, and neighbors? This was God's sixth day of work. Maybe it should be ours too. On Saturday, we could banish loneliness.

As you read this book, consider its premise, and absorb its content, my hope is that by enacting God's path through the first week of creation, each day you will more closely reflect the holy, creative work that God has in mind for you.

Using the Book

While you might want to read this book from the first chapter to last in the ordinary way, the premise of this book entertains the possibility that, embedded within the Biblical Creation narrative, God might be suggesting a particular discipleship practice we ought to pursue on Mondays in particular, then another one on Tuesdays, and yet another on Wednesdays, Thursdays, Fridays, and Saturdays, before worship and rest on Sundays.

As you see in the Contents, the book is divided into days of the week, each with ten chapters each. Consider reading the first chapter under the heading Monday on a Monday, then on Tuesday, read the first entry under Tuesday, then go on from there to each day of the week, turning back to the next Monday entry only when Monday comes back around again.

Reading the book in this way represents a way to truly follow creation. I hope if you do this, day after day, week after week, the practice will help you develop the habit of taking up in some measure the beautiful work God took up each day as referenced in the opening pages of Genesis.

Monday

Light

And God said, "Let there be light," and there was light . . . . And there was evening, and there was morning—the first day. (Genesis 1:3, 5, NIV)

The Courage to Encourage

Take heart! (John 16:33)

As soon as I arrived for my first year in college, I was assigned to a small orientation group with seven other freshmen like myself, along with two friendly seniors who knew their way around campus. Over the next several days, we all got to know one another as the seniors led us through a series of discussions about where we were from, the upcoming challenges of college life, and what we might come to expect both in our classes and in the dorms.

Looking back on it, it's all sort of a blur, but what I remember most about that week was that at its conclusion, the seniors—having come to know us pretty well—took the time to write personal notes of encouragement to each of us as we officially entered this new chapter of our lives. That note made a big difference to me. The writers of this memorable note began with a brief observation then began to encourage me. They wrote that I seemed to be a quiet person but said I shouldn't hesitate to speak up because I often seemed like I had something considered and important to say. I'm sure the two people who wrote this short note don't remember it at all. While I can't track with any precision how their words changed my life, I believe they did. After all, I still remember them almost forty years later.

It's not unusual for youth camps, weekend retreats, and church outings to conclude with some sort of exercise or ceremony in which heartfelt words—friend to friend, counselor to camper, parent to child—are exchanged. Why? Because we all know that authentic, thoughtful, and generous words of encouragement are some of the most powerful catalysts in the world. They reliably move our minds and change our perspectives, fortifying and inspiring us with confidence and a particularly energizing brand of courage. I think such encouragement is one of the main ways God moves in the world, using human voices to transmit both the words God desires us to hear and the spirit with which God wants us to live. We thirst for this voice in our lives.

I have a theory that one of the contributing factors to the division in our culture is our desire for reassurance. We work hard in a complex, high-velocity world, and—often exhausted at day's end—we all just want to be reassured and encouraged with a message that everything, as we see it, is going to be all right. For this reason, we retreat almost exclusively to places where we know we can find fortifying encouragement—places where we can count on being offered confidence to keep going back out there day after day. When you think about it, that's a pretty reasonable thing to want and need. But what if we could be recharged in a healthier way? What if, at the beginning of every week, we made a point to encourage each other more? What if we decided on Monday mornings that those we encounter will leave our presence with a thoughtful and meaningful word of encouragement tailored to their circumstances?

One of the reasons I think we require special notes and capstone ceremonies to provide this profound gift to one another is because it takes special courage to offer it. It's hard to tell someone earnestly what you see inside them—what you think they could be. We're often afraid to be serious with each other, so we hold back. But we shouldn't.

If you've experienced powerful and meaningful encouragement, then take stock of your sphere of influence. Maybe there's a child, a grandchild, a youth whom you coach, a particular student you teach, someone you mentor or employ. Perhaps there's a kid in your school a few grades behind you. Do you have some influence in your neighborhood, or within your apartment complex? Use it to offer encouragement to someone within your circle of concern.

How many times each day, each week, each month do you have the opportunity to transmit courage to another person with a well-timed, well-tuned word, yet, for whatever reason, you've held back?

God, whom do you want me to encourage on Monday? Jesus told his disciples, "Take heart!" Teach me what I should say. May I have the courage to speak. Amen.

Mercy

Mercy!

—*Gertie Warren Funderburk*

One of my lasting memories of my grandmother, Gertie Warren Funderburk, is how she responded when I did something original—like sink a fish hook in my finger or carry a bushel of pecans from the yard into her house in my stretched-out T-shirt. She'd trill out a deep breath in a weary whistle and say, "Mercy!" Back then, the only time I reached for this old-timey word myself was when gamely wrestling with my older brother, David. Hopelessly pinned and exhausted, I used it most reluctantly when obliged to surrender the match.

Recently though, I was giving a talk at an assisted-living facility, and my fifth grade teacher, whom I hadn't seen in forty-five years, was in the audience. I remembered that while I was familiar with the meaning of the word "mercy," it wasn't until a particular incident in Mrs. Charlotte Matula's elementary school class that I felt the full force of its power.

My childhood friend Sean Daichman and I were avid fans of the old *Bob Newhart Show,* and we were reliving a humorous episode of it during Mrs. Matula's lecture one afternoon, becoming so tickled that we couldn't stop laughing. After we interrupted her lesson for about the third time, Mrs. Matula brought the class to a halt and sent us outside, promising punishment as soon as she reached a good stopping point. Expecting to be sent directly to the principal's office, Sean and I grew solemn upon our exit from the classroom. It looked for all the world like that would happen as Mrs. Matula, looking very stern, joined us outside her room.

When asked about our misbehavior, Sean, a bit less anxious than I was, recounted the details of the *Bob Newhart Show*, thinking its sheer hilarity might prove exculpatory. For my part, I just stood there sorely distressed. Maybe Mrs. Matula felt some sympathy for me given my worried expression, or maybe she too was a Bob Newhart fan, but what she did next changed things: she trilled out a deep breath of her own and told Sean and me to return to class, insisting only that we re-gather ourselves, refrain from further antics, and telegraph to the rest of the class a sense that we'd been punished quite severely.

Mercy.

At the conclusion of my talk a few weeks ago, I approached Mrs. Matula and told her how this experience had stuck with me, but she didn't seem to recall it. Maybe she didn't remember because it was how she commonly dealt with such conduct. To her, maybe such acts of mercy weren't unusual. I expect this was probably the case, as four decades on, she appeared to be a woman full of grace—so full of grace that she didn't seem surprised by the story. It was just her way of doing business. She'd stopped counting or even recalling such emblematic acts. They'd simply become a part of her nature.

To become more graceful seems a worthy goal, but how might we go about it? How do we cultivate a more graceful temperament, a more grace-filled approach to life? I think the answer is tied up in this notion of mercy. If grace is the picture we want to see when we look at ourselves, then acts of mercy are like the pixels that form and define the image we seek.

Or think of it this way—how often does the result we deserve for our errors, our sins, our deliberate coloring outside the lines come to us? Think about all we get away with, all the times we outrace karma, avoiding our just deserts. How many times have we failed to live up to the standards we know we should? How many times have we acted negligently, even recklessly, without bad results? Think of all you've done and left undone without true justice levied. God is graceful because God acts with mercy. Mercy at most every turn.

The lesson might be this: we build lives of grace by daily piling up acts of mercy. If you're angry at someone, forgive them. Do it today. If someone offends you or acts rudely to you, either devoid of or with complete self-awareness, do your best to let it go. Let it go today. It's only through our dispensation of individual, daily offerings of mercy that we become people of grace. I don't think there's any other way.

God, may we build up lives of grace by dispensing acts of Monday mercy. Amen.

3

Humility

I try to hide my efforts, wishing my work to have a light joyousness of springtime which never lets anyone suspect the labors it has cost me.
—Henri Matisse

One of my favorite stories involves a husband and wife walking through a museum featuring a modern art exhibit. The husband glances at one of the canvases, shakes his head ruefully about what he perceives to be the childish simplicity of the painting, and says, "I could've done *that*." His wife looks at the piece then back at him and replies, "Then why didn't you?" Her response suggests how we might think more deeply, not only about contemporary art but also about one another's work and effort.

During Henri Matisse's remarkable six-decade artistic career, he worked in a wide array of mediums—drawing, painting, sculpture, bronze relief, stained glass, decorative set designs for ballet performances, lithographs, etchings, murals for the interiors of homes, and book illustrations.[1] In the early 1900s, he began to experiment with a new kind of brushwork that gave rise to a primitive yet vibrant look to his canvases. He started selecting wild new combinations of expressive colors for his work—colors that reacted dramatically

---

1. Magdalena Dabrowski, "Henri Matisse (1869–1954)," *Heilbrunn Timeline of Art History*, Metmuseum.org, http://www.metmuseum.org/toah/hd/mati/hd_mati.htm (October 2004).

with each other on the canvas.² Next, he began to use bolder lines to outline his subjects, moving away from the softer contours favored at the height of the Impressionism movement years before. Using these innovations, Matisse learned to direct the flow of a viewer's eyes, creating a kind of joyful motion, exuberance, and spontaneity in his paintings.³ While some were critical of his work, calling it simple and even childlike, the new techniques represented an evolution of his artistic style that emerged from his study, experience, and imagination combined with the labor-intensive brand of craftsmanship he regularly employed in all of his work. "I try to hide my efforts," Matisse said, "wishing my work to have a light joyousness of springtime which never lets anyone suspect the labors it has cost me."⁴

Decades later, in his seventies, Matisse was unable to work long hours at an easel because his eyesight and mobility were failing. On one miserable day at work, he took fabric shears and snipped out the shape of a bird from some paper in his studio.⁵ He asked one of his studio assistants to pin it up on the wall to hide a stain.⁶ Deciding that he liked how it looked, he cut out more, and then more. Soon he had his assistants washing large sheets of paper in a range of colors. He cut them carefully into all sorts of whimsical shapes and sizes and directed his assistants, now balancing on ladders, to affix them *just so* onto the walls of his studio with tailor pins.⁷ Some of the shapes looked like flying, falling figures (*The Fall of Icarus*, 1947), others appeared to be leaping divers and splashing swimmers (*The Swimming Pool*, 1952), and still others were merely suggestive of gusting

---

2. Ibid.

3. Ibid.

4. "Famous Henri Matisse Quotes," *Henri Matisse: Biography, Artworks, & Quotes*, www.henrimatisse.org/henri-matisse-quotes.jsp.

5. Karl D. Buchberg et al., *Henri Matisse: The Cut-Outs*, illus. ed. (New York: Museum of Modern Art, 2014).

6. Holland Cotter, "Wisps from an Old Man's Dreams," *New York Times*, October 9, 2014.

7. Ibid.

clouds or shooting stars set high in the heavens or fish, algae, and coral deep under the sea.[8]

If Matisse had not invented a new art form, he had done something close to it. Described by one writer as "not quite painting, not quite sculpture, and not even really permanent,"[9] Matisse's compositions were rearranged and reworked until he was satisfied, and then the arrangements were transferred from his studio using an elaborate tracing process to then be affixed with special adhesives directly to the walls of museums, homes, or other exhibit spaces.[10] Simple yet sublime, the cut-outs, as he called them, were in the end something only Matisse—with his experience, with his skill, with even his scars—could have done.

As he was kinder and more patient than some others with his level of genius, I have to think that if Matisse had been eavesdropping on the exchange between the couple in that modern art gallery, he would have gently told the man that what he was looking at probably wasn't so simple to create, that it resulted from a good deal of skill, training, experience, thought, hardship, and long hours of trial and error. He might even have added that sometimes what's hard to do might give off the sense that it's easy, even when it's not. And that while everyone is entitled to an opinion and the right to criticize, before doing so—before passing judgment—a good and humble question to ask is, *Honestly, could I do any better?*

> *God, humility is a kind of light to cast out into the world. Help me today to better consider, appreciate, and value the work others do. Amen.*

---

8. Buchberg et al., *Henri Matisse: The Cut-Outs*, 104, 222.
9. Holland, "Wisps."
10. Buchberg et al., *Henri Matisse: The Cut-Outs*, 12.

Forbearance

Bear with one another . . . . (Colossians 3:13a)

When I was in elementary school, I had to take speech. Not the class in which you're instructed on how to give a public talk but the one in which you're taught how to pronounce your letters properly. You see, I had a stormy relationship with the letter R. I was solid when it came to important playground phrases like "Red Rover, Red Rover" or with the lyrics to "Row, Row, Row Your Boat." I was also capable of enunciating the names of lead characters from stories like Little Red Riding Hood, Rumpelstiltskin, and Rapunzel. Trickier for me were words with an R in the middle or at the end. Like the word "word" for instance. Or the word "or." I had issues with "were" and "bird" and with "bread" and "thread." As you might imagine, this was a tough beat for a kid named Greg Funderburk, which from kindergarten through second grade I rendered as "Gweg Fund-a-book." It wasn't pretty.

So off I went one day to speech therapy with my friend Mac, who had a similar problem with his R's. Mac's last name, by the way, was Greer, also unfortunate under the circumstances. We left all our classmates and some of our self-esteem behind and headed down the hall to a small room nestled in an out-of-the-way corner of the school. Inside, we found a few chairs, a table, and walls adorned with big colorful letters. However, a closer look also revealed a series of clinical illustrations, each depicting the proper embouchure and correct position of the tongue required to make the sounds of all the pesky alphabet letters in accordance with prevailing standards. A kind woman greeted us and introduced herself as Mrs. Joseph. We reciprocated, telling her our names, and thereby making clear the scope of the task at hand. Then, under her patient tutelage, we began taking up the vexatious letter R with one another.

Eventually, with Mrs. Joseph's help, Mac and I overcame our problems and moved beyond the ordeal. The key with R's, in case you're wondering, is to place the sides of the tongue against one's molars and make a distinct yet subtle growling sound. "Rrrrrr."

What I recall most vividly, beyond our triumph over the eighteenth letter of the alphabet, was how Mac and I, despite our lingual deficiencies and without a bit of self-awareness, used to make fun of the kids who had a hard time with the letter S. A lispy *th* sound would invariably emerge from their mouths instead of the slippery letter S. As second graders, Mac and I told ourselves that perhaps we sounded like toddlers sometimes with our R's, but at least we didn't sound like babies the way the S kids did.

I tell you this story to illustrate something common—not just in insecure, immature children as we were—but a problem that persists in all of us. We all have issues, shortcomings, and deficits that vex us, but because they're *our* things, *our* problems, we're sensitive to them and about them. However, when others are afflicted with similar problems, we often fail to exhibit the same measure of sensitivity. Likewise, we're usually quite attuned to how others bother or offend us but not nearly so well-attuned about what we might do that bothers or offends them.

At the core of Jesus's Sermon on the Mount and at the center of Paul's letters to both the Colossians and the Ephesians is the idea that we ought to strive to put ourselves in the shoes of others. God seems to impress upon us time and time again in Scripture that we ought to make wide and graceful allowances for each other's faults, especially in view of our own. That is, we ought to bear with one another, excuse each other's mistakes, ill temperaments, and blind spots, and—here's the hardest part—forego the emotional satisfaction that's readily available to us when we put others down for the same faults, mistakes, and guile we ourselves keenly embody. While criticizing others reliably produces an addictive elation inside of us, it comes at the terrible expense of corroding our souls.

I guarantee you that it won't be hard to find something in others this week that bothers or offends you. But when it inevitably happens, instead of looking at the other person with such a critical eye and at yourself with such a graceful one, try saving the grace for them instead. Thanks to Mrs. Joseph, I can properly pronounce the divine word that encompasses this sacred idea: *Forbearance*.

God, help me today and this week to remember the importance of forbearance—wide and graceful allowances all around for the faults of others, especially in view of my own. Amen.

A Lasting Good

The true measure of all our actions is how long the good in them lasts.

—Queen Elizabeth II

Queen Elizabeth II was the first monarch in the long and storied history of the British empire to serve her people and country for seven full decades. She was only twenty-five years old when her father, King George VI, died in 1952 and she acceded to the throne. She passed away in September 2022 at ninety-six years of age as the longest-serving female head of state in the history of the world.[1]

Queen Elizabeth lived a remarkable life, reigning through a period of tumultuous political change in a time of significant cultural evolution and technological advancement. She also endured a number of episodes of acute family trauma. However, because she gave interviews only rarely, and it has always been against the prevailing convention to ask a royal personage to reveal her views on public matters, relatively little was known of the queen's personal feelings about the world or her place in it. Nevertheless, even before a compelling television series called *The Crown* was produced concerning the events of her life, it was clear that she had always been a serious person who executed her solemn duties with honor and dignity, placing the needs

---

1. Willem Marx, "Queen Elizabeth II, longest-serving monarch in British history, dies at 96," *NPR*, September 8, 2022, www.npr.org/2022/09/08/1121865505/queen-elizabeth-ii-longest-serving-monarch-in-british-history-dies-at-96.

of state above her personal desires. It is also clear that she accrued great wisdom over her long life in the public spotlight.

In 2014, speaking to British and French dignitaries at a state banquet on the seventieth anniversary of D-Day, Queen Elizabeth recalled the loss of those who so courageously fought on the beaches of Normandy. Then, in expressing both a deep appreciation for their sacrifice and earnest gratitude for the unity and abiding friendship between Great Britain and France, she dispensed this brilliant thought: "The true measure of all our actions is how long the good in them lasts."[2]

In such a high-velocity age, with a world of instant news where instantaneous judgments are expected rather than discouraged, we often measure things shortsightedly. We esteem things that soon melt away like cotton candy. The queen's words instead encourage us to weigh events and actions not by their immediate or apparent effect or by the acclaim they might generate initially but rather by how the good in them might echo down and persist into the future—that is, how they might influence for good the trajectory of lives well beyond our own.

Heroic acts such as those of the brave soldiers, sailors, and airmen who gave their lives to establish a beachhead that liberated a whole continent from tyranny are densely packed with durable good. Such good effects cascade through time, and have changed the course of history and the lives of untold millions.

But what about us? Certainly, most of us won't ever be called to make such a spectacular sacrifice, but we can still hold this same measuring stick next to our own lives. What most reliably creates a good that lasts is the very thing that prompted the queen's words on that occasion in the first place—the notion of *sacrifice*. And while it arose in her in a less dramatic form than in a courageous soldier storming a fortified beach (she enlisted and served in the Auxiliary Territorial Service, the women's branch of the British Army, and

---

2. Robert Hardman, "Everything we do, we do for the young . . .," *Daily Mail*, June 6, 2014, www.dailymail.co.uk/news/article-2650968/The-woman-personifies-Keep-Calm-Carry-On-French-presidents-toast-Queen-French-AND-English-banquet-mark-D-Day.html.

learned to fix and drive trucks during the war)—in the queen's devotion to duty and her people for more than seventy years, sacrifice was a concept she certainly knew something about.

Her observation suggests that whether we are soldiers, first responders, faithful public servants, dutiful mothers, devoted fathers, children caring for aging parents, steadfast friends to friends in need, or simply good neighbors, sacrifice produces durability in the good we do. We know this intuitively, for it is written on our hearts. Think about it. The notion of sacrifice moves us in story, in film, in history, in our relationships, and throughout our lives. We need to look no further than the gospel to see that this is true. What we're willing to sacrifice—*of ourselves for the benefit of others*—is what produces lasting good in the world.

Do you want your life to produce a good that lasts? Then ask yourself what you can sacrifice from your own life today for the good of another. It's a good measuring stick from a wise ruler.

> *God, may I take proper measure of the lasting effect of what I'm doing in the world and become willing to sacrifice more of myself for others today. Amen.*

Our Very Best

There's always someone in the stands... who's seeing me play for the first time, or someone who may be seeing me for the only time or for the last time.
—Joe DiMaggio

I got to see Willie Mays, Bob Gibson, Tom Seaver, Johnny Bench, Hank Aaron, and, my all-time favorite, Roberto Clemente at the Astrodome growing up. Looking back on it, I have to hand it to my dad for taking us—my brother David, a teenager in the Big Brother program named John, and me—to so many Astros games. Dad had a taxing job, and while I know he liked going to the games, being with us, and serving as a mentor to John, those must have been long days: leaving the office, getting us ready and into the car, picking up John, driving to the stadium, parking, settling us into our seats and feeding us, and then tolerating our general rambunctiousness with our popcorn-container megaphones and our many questions about the game. Finally, after likely experiencing a lopsided loss, he'd corral us all up again, struggle to keep us together on the bustling exit ramps on the way out, fight all the traffic again, get John home, then put David and me to bed. The energy. The commitment. *Well done, Dad.*

It certainly wasn't my dad's fault that I never got to see Joe DiMaggio play. I was born too late and he was in the other league anyway, but from all I've read and seen on film, DiMaggio was one of a kind. Whether his team, the Yankees, were up five runs in the opening week of the season, down five runs in the heat of the summer, or locked in a one-run pitchers' duel with the pennant on the line, DiMaggio played exactly the same way. All out. All the time. If DiMaggio hit a lazy fly to the outfield that was sure to be caught, he'd gallop full speed to first base anyway, touch the bag, and be on his way to second as the fielder circled under it to make the easy catch. Likewise, on defense, DiMaggio would dash, then crash headlong into the outfield wall no matter the score or circumstance if a catch could possibly be made. That's just how he played. Every game. Every inning. Every time up.

When asked, he explained, "There's always someone in the stands, some kid in the stands, who's seeing me play for the first time or someone who may be seeing me for the only time or for the last time. I owe them my best effort."[1]

This is true for all of us in a sense. While you are on a less dramatic stage than the field at Yankee Stadium, every day someone sees you for the first time. Maybe it's a kid in the stands, so to speak. Perhaps it's a younger person who's subconsciously looking for a mentor, a model for how to live. Or perhaps it's someone you'll meet today and only encounter once in your life. In the waiting room at the dentist's office. In line at the DMV. Next to you on a flight. This is the only time your lives will ever intersect. Or maybe today marks the last time you'll closely connect with someone you've known for a while. Will these encounters mean anything? Will any of these folks' lives be enriched by crossing paths with you? What impression will you leave with each of them?

It is important to think about who and what receives our attention, but the quality of attention we give is important too. There's always someone in the stands watching you play for the first time, for the only time, for the last time. What are they witnessing? What are they seeing when they see you?

Maybe just the thought of approaching life like this—always on, always on stage—seems exhausting. And you might say Joltin' Joe

---

1. Boyd Matheson, "Here's to you, Joe DiMaggio, for showing us how it's done," *KSL NewsRadio*, June 10, 2021, kslnewsradio.com/1950118/opinion-joe-dimaggio-shows-us-how-its-done/.

DiMaggio only had to exert maximum effort for a few hours a day. No one can live their whole life that way. That is true enough, but consider this: for the sake of the kid who's watching you today; for the sake of the person you'll encounter once—this week only—and never again; for the sake of the friend or the colleague who offers you the chance at a meaningful conversation; for the sake of our God who gave us life and every blessing we enjoy—don't ever just phone it in. Not ever. Not a single day. Especially not today.

God, help me offer my best to everything and to everyone I encounter on this day. I owe them that. I owe You that. Amen.

Empathy

There's nothing that can replace the absence of someone dear to us.

—*Dietrich Bonhoeffer,*
Letters and Papers from Prison

"Patricia Ann Funderburk lived a life of grace and cheer with the full heart of a selfless servant. She was born on October 8, 1935, in Hominy, Oklahoma, and passed away peacefully at home with her family on December 8, 2013." That's how I began my mother's obituary when I undertook to write it ten years ago. I will share a little more:

> Upon graduating from Kansas University, Patricia obtained her license in occupational therapy before coming to Houston to work for the Texas Institute for Rehabilitation and Research. At TIRR, she worked with those stricken by polio, burn victims, and other young disabled patients, providing them not only practical assistance and training, but hope.
>
> In Houston, she met Weldon Funderburk and they married on December 9, 1961, and began a family together. Patricia was a kind and patient mother and a loving wife who inspired her children to care for others in practical ways, setting an example for them as an ardent volunteer and joyful caregiver. She carried a casual loveliness into whatever environment she entered, always looking with intention for those who needed help, hope, or a kind word.

She painted, created exuberant, colorful collages, and enjoyed singing, traveling, and being a part of her children's sports and school activities. She made a number of lifelong friends serving many years in the Special Education Department at Tallowood Baptist Church where she was a favorite of the students.

Pat was diagnosed with neurological difficulties and early onset dementia from which she suffered courageously for over two decades and will be remembered for relentlessly facing adversity with a sweetness of spirit that exemplified her entire life and inspired all those who loved her dearly.

A few years ago, I led a graveside service for a gifted doctor on the grounds of Houston's most beautiful cemetery, after which his widow, Miriam, sent me a memorable letter offering her thanks for honoring her husband. Miriam in many ways reminded me of my own mother. Like mine, she was the sort of mother who would wake her kids up in the morning with a happy tune. Or she might try to start a sing-along on a commercial bus. There's something irrepressible about a singing mom. It's embarrassing in the moment, but with a little distance, it's endearing and beautiful. Also like my mother, Miriam was extravagantly gracious. She extended the benefit of the doubt to anyone who cut her off in traffic, not concluding that they were rude but instead accounting for their bad behavior by assuming that they were high. It didn't surprise me when I was told Miriam had the ability to float in a pool effortlessly. She had a transcendent lightness about her. She loved art and growing flowers. And she loved putting words together well, which brings me back to the elevating letter she sent me.

Miriam's note, apart from it being among the kindest letters I've ever received, also included edifying guidance about both navigating and understanding the nature of grief. They're the words of Dietrich Bonhoeffer, the Lutheran pastor who was imprisoned then killed in a German concentration camp at the end of World War II. After I read the note from Miriam, Bonhoeffer's insight soon began to shape how I interacted with those who had lost loved ones. Ruthlessly genuine, beautifully real, and true whether we like it or not, his wisdom is fully grounded in the inevitable nature of human love and close relationships. Ever since, the words have helped me offer a deeper empathy to those who are in sorrow and to understand and process my own losses as well. Here's what Miriam told me Bonhoeffer said:

> There is nothing that can replace the absence of someone dear to us, and one should not even attempt to do so. One must simply hold out and endure it. At first that sounds very hard, but at the same time it is also a great comfort. For to the extent the emptiness truly remains unfilled one remains connected to the other person through it. It is wrong to say that God fills the emptiness. God in no way fills it but much more leaves it precisely unfilled and thus helps us preserve—even in pain—the authentic relationship. Furthermore, the more beautiful and fuller the remembrances, the more difficult the separation. But gratitude transforms the torment of memory into silent joy. One bears what was lovely in the past not as a thorn but as a precious gift deep within, a hidden treasure of which one can always be certain.[1]

God, help me to hold the light of empathy upwards today. And move me gently toward a deeper kind of joy—the mysterious but indelible sort that resides within memory alone. Amen.

---

1. See Dietrich Bonhoeffer, *Letters and Papers from Prison*, updated ed. (Chicago: Touchstone, 1997).

A Renegade Good Will

Of course, none of this is likely, but it's also not impossible. It just depends on what you want to consider.
—David Foster Wallace

I had a couple of friends back in college who got a kick out of telling semi-credible tall tales about each other to unsuspecting acquaintances at parties. For instance, in conversation, one might point across the room to the other and suggest his friend's lifelong dream was to become a professional bowler. At the same time, the other guy might be in deep dialogue with someone else, noting that his friend over there calls square dances outside of town every weekend. The exchanges were always dryly delivered with just enough backstory for them to seem plausible—or at least not impossible.

How we go about judging what's possible, what's plausible, and what's not—both in general and about one another—is an interesting process, but Scripture gives us some guidance. We're instructed that grace and good will aren't things to be calibrated to the truth about people. They're not to be doled out according to performance or preference, but freely offered.

In the novel *Great Expectations*, Charles Dickens's protagonist, Pip, works with John Wemmick, a bill collector whose job requires him to do some harsh things. Pip observes that Wemmick has an "air of knowing something to everybody else's disadvantage" and develops a negative impression of him.[1] However, one day Wemmick asks Pip to stay the weekend with him at his home. As they leave the office and then the city, Pip notices that Wemmick's whole bearing changes. At Wemmick's home, Pip discovers his host cares for his elderly father, whom Wemmick kindly calls "Aged Parent" or, more fondly still, "Aged P."[2] Wemmick prepares a lovely dinner for all of them, and when he awakes later, Pip hears Wemmick cleaning Pip's own boots. Next, Pip looks out the window to see Wemmick tending his garden with Aged P at his side. Pip later learns that Wemmick is engaged to marry the lovely Miss Skiffins, whom he refers to as the source of all joy in his life.[3] Pip thought Wemmick was stern, cynical, and dull. Instead, he's genial, warm, and impressively interesting.

The writers of the long-running television sitcom *Parks and Recreation* seem to have created an echo of Mr. Wemmick in Garry Gergich, who works in the Pawnee Parks and Recreation Department where the series is set. Garry appears to be a boring, bumbling, middle-aged man. All the other characters tease and even mock him. However, as the show unfolds over the course of several years, whenever one of the other characters is thrown into a situation with Garry alone, they're surprised to find him incredibly charming, agile, and interesting. Garry, it turns out, is a gifted pianist, an amateur inventor, a terrific chef, and a skilled artist. In one episode, he quietly creates a mural in an alcove of City Hall meticulously composed of tiny pictures of the town's citizens. Later, we discover he has a devoted wife (played by Christie Brinkley) and three beautiful daughters.[4]

Author David Foster Wallace gave a commencement address to the 2005 graduates of Kenyon College.[5] I reread it at least once a year. It's that good. In it, Wallace submits that almost every minute

---

1. Charles Dickens, *Great Expectations* (Ware, England: Wordsworth Classics, 1992).
2. Ibid.
3. Ibid.
4. *Parks and Recreation*, created by Greg Daniels and Mike Schur, NBC, 2009–2015.
5. David Foster Wallace, *This Is Water* (New York: Little, Brown & Company, 2009).

of every day, we have a choice regarding whether to treat those we encounter charitably or not. Wallace says we can proceed on our default setting, doling out our good will only to those we like and care about when it suits us, or we can decide to treat every sacred, created human being with intentional kindness—something we could call renegade good will. For instance, instead of assuming the worst of that driver who cut us off in traffic, Wallace proposes we seriously consider the possibility that he might be trying to get his injured son to the hospital. Maybe it's us who are in *his* way. Perhaps that lady screaming at her kid in the checkout line isn't usually like this, but she's been up three nights in a row holding the hand of her husband who is dying from bone cancer.

In the end, Wallace humbly encourages us to consider being a little less arrogant about what we think we know of one another and consider what else might be plausible or at least not impossible. Creating such charitable backstories about everyone we encounter represents a lot of imaginative, even fictional work, but, then again, Jesus never said living out the Sermon on the Mount was easy.

God, may I offer a renegade brand of good will to all I encounter today. Amen.

Gratitude

If this isn't nice, what is?

—Kurt Vonnegut,
Speech to Butler University graduates, May 11, 1996

Every year as spring moves into summer, new classes of bright-eyed students cross the stage, then fling their curiously shaped hats high into the air with great energy. A few weeks after this occurs, some enterprising publication or website gathers up all the sage and inspiring commencement remarks offered to these graduates and their dewy-eyed parents and chooses the best of them.

Every year, the lists of the "Best Commencement Speeches" are sprinkled with names we know: Olympic champions, political leaders, captains of industry, Pulitzer Prize winners, and some of our culture's more thoughtful celebrities. Tom Hanks spoke at Harvard. John McEnroe at Stanford. Oprah at Tennessee State. Six-time Olympic medalist Jackie Joyner-Kersee at the University of Illinois. New York Times columnist Bret Stephens provided the remarks at his alma mater, the University of Chicago while actor Martin Sheen spoke at Loyola-Marymount. Jazz musician Wynton Marsalis addressed the students at Michigan, and Kevin Feige, president of Marvel Studios, gave the commencement address at the University of Southern California. I expect they all brought something novel to the table. But none of them is Kurt Vonnegut.

Author Kurt Vonnegut was regularly invited to speak at college graduations, addressing students at schools like Rice, Chicago,

Syracuse, and Butler beginning in the 1960s when his first novel, *Slaughterhouse Five*, was published. The invitations continued to mount until the time of his death in 2007. Vonnegut spoke at so many graduation ceremonies that, posthumously in 2013, some of his best were gathered and turned into a book titled *If This Isn't Nice, What Is? Advice to the Young*.[1] Dan Wakefield, novelist, screenwriter, and author of several books on Christian spirituality, selected the nine speeches and penned an introduction to the volume. In it, Wakefield wrote that while Vonnegut was an underground hero of sorts to a generation of young students, he was also a "counter-counter-cultural figure," often satirizing the facile answers that a variety of new-age gurus of the time were offering regarding paths to peace and so-called enlightenment. In place of the usual ramblings presented at many graduations, Vonnegut's commencement messages—presented always in his unique conversational tone with neither platitude nor cant—pointed young graduates in a different direction. True joy and happiness, he suggested, was most reliably found simply through living with extraordinary kindness. Though an atheist, in one message Vonnegut called Jesus's expressions of mercy in the Sermon on the Mount "the only good idea we have had so far. Perhaps," he added, "we'll get another good idea by and by—and then we will have two good ideas."[2] Focusing on gratitude, in a commencement speech he gave in his hometown of Indianapolis, Indiana, at Butler University in 1996, he offered the graduates this advice:

> My Uncle Alex Vonnegut, an insurance salesman who lived at 5033 North Pennsylvania Avenue, taught me something very important. He said that when things are going really well we should be sure to notice it. He was talking about very simple occasions, not great victories. Maybe drinking lemonade under a shade tree, or smelling the aroma of a bakery, or fishing, or listening to music coming from a concert hall while standing outside, or dare

---

1. Kurt Vonnegut, *If This Isn't Nice, What Is?* Speeches selected and introduction by Dan Wakefield (New York: Seven Stories Press, 2013).
2. Ibid., xv.

I say, after a kiss. He told me that it was important at such times to say out loud, *"If this isn't nice, what is?"*[3]

This seems fairly easy and certainly worth doing, as is remembering another piece of Vonnegut's wisdom that emerges from this terrific little book of his collected commencement addresses. "The function of the artist," Vonnegut said, "*is to make people like life better than before.*" When he was later asked if this was possible, he replied, "Yes, the Beatles did it."[4]

A graduation ceremony is a "commencement" because, though it's the end of one sort of season, it marks the beginning of a new one. As set out into a new week, it might not be a bad idea to recognize this task of making life better for others isn't just for artists but for each one of us. And if we're going to embark on a fresh new course that involves trying to make people we encounter simply *like life better*, recognizing and acknowledging our own *"If this isn't nice, what is?"* moments might be a good place to commence the project.

> *God, as I begin to better recognize the small, sweet moments of everyday life right in front of me today, help me to gratefully commence trying to make people like life better than they did before. Amen.*

---

3. Ibid., 115.
4. Ibid., ix.

10

A New Dawn

One day the sun will come out—you might not even notice straight away, it'll be that faint.
—Brooklyn, *2015*

Not too long ago, my wife, Kelly, and I took our youngest son, Charlie, to college, and saying goodbye to him as he entered into a new phase of his life triggered some deeply etched memories. Trips we took when the kids were little. First days of elementary school, middle school, high school. Playing Little League games and watching old movies together as a family.

From an early age, Charlie has had a way of underlining the pain inherent in seasons of transition. For instance, at just four or five years old, when Charlie was especially down about leaving preschool and his classmates behind, Kelly asked him about it. He replied that he was sad because this was the last time he'd be friends with many of those people. We tried to convince him otherwise, but he was right. Time just carries us along.

I recently learned that the word "nostalgia" first entered our lexicon, not as a way to refer to the wistful feeling we get about our memories, but as a medical term. A Swiss physician named Johannes Hofer coined the term in 1688, combining the Greek words *nostos*, meaning "homecoming," with *algos*, meaning "pain."[1] His explanation of the malady he named referred to the emotional suffering and

---

1. Julie Beck, "When Nostalgia Was a Disease," *Atlantic*, August 14, 2013.

constellation of physical symptoms that yearning for the past often brings. That is to say, the notion of nostalgia was originally more associated with the pain certain memories cause than with the beauty they might evoke.

One of the memorable movies our family watched together years ago was called *Brooklyn*, a film about a vulnerable yet steely teenager named Eilis Lacey who leaves her home and family in rural Ireland in the 1950s to come to America, landing on Ellis Island before settling in Brooklyn.[2] Lonely, isolated, and conflicted, Eilis bears the full weight and despair of homesickness as she makes a new life for herself in a strange and far-flung place. Toward the end of the film, Eilis offers another young immigrant arriving in New York City this advice:

> You'll feel so homesick that you'll want to die, and there's nothing you can do about it apart from endure it. But you will, and it won't kill you. And one day the sun will come out—you might not even notice straight away—it'll be that faint. And then you'll catch yourself thinking about something or someone who has no connection with the past . . . . And you'll realize that this is where your life is.

The actress playing Eilis, the talented Saoirse Ronan, delivered the line with great empathy but without sentimentality. Warmly, and in a way that lent enormous beauty and hope to the exchange, she transmitted the notion that the sadness homesickness casts over a person is more often transcended than conquered. But because of this—because this is how it's most commonly overcome—rather than taking something from our souls, what we endure instead somehow expands our souls.

Whether you're facing down the pain of homesickness, the anxiety of transition, the uncertainty of a liminal season, or the deep sorrow of terrible loss, one of the most difficult things about suffering is how hard it is to believe that it will ever end, fade, or even change.

---

2. *Brooklyn*, directed by John Crowley, written by Nick Hornby and Colm Toíbín, 20th Century Studios, Lionsgate Films, and Mongrel Media, 2015.

And yet, ". . . one day the sun will come out—you might not even notice straight away, it'll be that faint . . . ."

And in that fleeting moment of recognition—when it finally occurs—take this new dawn, this little glimmer of a feeling, though faint and alloyed still with great pain, and hold it up to God, knowing that through the strange alchemy of time and experience, the alloy changes, and changes, and changes.

> *God, help me today at the beginning of the week to hold my pain upward in hope, aware of how it might change—and change me. May it become holy. Amen.*

Tuesday

Order

And God said, "Let there be a vault between the waters to separate water from water." . . . And there was evening, and there was morning—the second day. (Genesis 1:6, 8)

Single-Tasking

This is the case. There are no other cases.
—*Frank Galvin,* The Verdict

I regularly listen to *The Rewatchables*, a podcast that light-heartedly revisits popular movies of the past, focusing on their power to entertain us even, perhaps especially, on a second viewing, or a third, or even a tenth. The show recently turned its listeners' attention to a 1982 movie called *The Verdict* in which Paul Newman plays Frank Galvin, once an up-and-coming lawyer who, after some misfortune, loses his wife and becomes an alcoholic ambulance-chaser barely able to scrape together a living for himself.[1] Out of pity, another attorney, Frank's friend Mickey, refers a medical malpractice lawsuit to him. It involves a young woman who has been left comatose after the delivery of her baby goes awry in the hospital. Frank will represent the woman and her family against the doctors and a hospital operated by the Catholic Diocese of Boston. The question of the doctors' negligence is at the heart of the case.

The Church's lawyers are formidable but offer Frank a settlement figure adequate to provide for the woman's future medical care. However, emotionally affected upon visiting her, convinced the doctors are responsible, and certain that he is simply being bought off to look the other way, Frank declines the offer. There are setbacks as the trial begins. The other side, playing dirty, entices

---

1. *The Verdict*, directed by Sidney Lumet, screenplay by David Mamet, 20th Century Studios, 1982.

Frank's expert witness to disappear. The judge is in the bag for the Diocese, undermining Frank at every turn. Everything that could go wrong does go wrong. Worst of all, as the trial advances, Frank discovers he is betrayed by a woman he has met. She has been spying on him, feeding information about his preparation and strategy to the Church's lawyers. Mickey, seeing all is lost, urges Frank to ask for a mistrial due to the ethical breaches by opposing counsel.

"There'll be other cases," Mickey tells him, trying to console him. In response, Frank bows his head. "No," he says. "This is the case. There are no other cases. This is the case. There are no other cases. This is the case." He says this mantra-like, with grave intensity. "There are no other cases."

With these words, Frank recommits to the matter before him with new single-mindedness, resourcefulness, and a renewed belief in the justice of his cause, eventually leading the film to its dramatic conclusion. I encourage you at least to watch Paul Newman's delivery of Frank's climactic closing argument—or rewatch as the case may be.

Frank's resolve, represented in these repeating lines, communicates the sort of singular focus needed to overcome the highest and most complex challenges life throws at us. We intuitively know that some things require not just our undivided attention but an almost superhuman focus on the sole matter at hand. On too many days, in too many circumstances, when perhaps the stakes aren't considered quite so high, we allow our attention to become so fragmented that there's no way we can offer our best to the thing or the person right before us. That is, we refuse—and it says a lot that this is even a word—to *single-task*.

The urge to multitask is often born from the feeling that we don't have enough time to do everything we want or need to do. This constant sense of time-impoverishment leads us to taking up the brilliant idea that we're perfectly capable of doing two or more things at once. However, no matter what we tell ourselves, we are really not capable of that. Neuroscientists who have studied this brilliant idea of ours tell us we're not really doing what we think we're doing anyway. That is, we're not really doing two things at once but rather switching back and forth between and across two networks and accepting in the bargain a significant cost—the degradation of our attention to both endeavors we're trying to do simultaneously.

Sure, we can probably make our way through most of life willingly shedding IQ points and emotional energy to these switching costs, mired in the habit of dividing and subdividing our attention like this, multitasking our way along. But it's not really offering our best to God with the *today* that God has blessed us with, and it's certainly an act of negligence when, with Christ's life as our standard, we only offer a part of ourselves to the person right before us. Let's not settle for that.

> *God, this is the today you've given me. There is no other today. With single focus, may I give to it—and to those before me—my full attention. Amen.*

Remove One

Before you leave the house, look in the mirror and remove one accessory.

—*Coco Chanel*

When you think of Chanel, if you think of Chanel at all, your mind might run to a picture of two interlocking C's forming a distinctive gold clasp that adorns one of the company's stylish black handbags. Or perhaps you might conjure up an image of an austere yet iconic black sans serif *Chanel No. 5* set against a clean white background and elegantly affixed to the front of a perfectly beveled perfume bottle.

Although the Chanel logo calls up notions of luxury and high fashion like only a handful of other internationally known brands, Gabrielle Chanel, the company's founder and namesake, came from humble beginnings. Her father peddled work garments on the streets and lived nomadically, traveling from town to town in France to sell his wares in the early 1880s.[1] Her mother was an overworked laundrywoman. The future fashion mogul herself was born in a charity hospital in 1883, grew up with five siblings in a crowded single-room home, and never attended school. Gabrielle's mother died when Gabrielle was only eleven.[2] Her father, unable to care for his family, sent his boys out to work and Gabrielle and her sisters to a nearby

---

1. Lisa Chaney, *Chanel: An Intimate Life* (London: Penguin, 2011).
2. Ibid.

orphanage.³ There, amid acute hardship and strict discipline, she learned to sew.

Never adopted, when she turned eighteen, Gabrielle moved into a boarding house for young Catholic women where she began to develop a talent for designing dashing and well-crafted hats.⁴ By her late twenties, she'd made a name for herself as a milliner, purchased a building in a fashionable district of Paris, and opened a small boutique. There, she expanded her line—creating clothing, accessories, and jewelry and experimenting with fragrances. Using her talent, compelling personality, and remarkable genius for self-invention, her company steadily grew. As it did, Chanel enlisted friends to tutor her in literature, art, music, and history. Now moving in elite circles of Parisian society, she created a sort of social and professional alter-ego for herself and took on the name "Coco."

In cut and construction, Coco Chanel's clothes were at once revolutionary and practical. She pared down her designs to the most basic forms, rarely tight yet rarely loose. Choosing materials with natural elasticity, she simplified the contours of her designs, delivering a look and a comfort women could—she said—laugh in. As her fashion sense continued to evolve aesthetically, she began to add subtle, tasteful ornamentation to her designs, synthesizing modernity with a classic timelessness—just enough but never too much. Her intuitive sense of harmony, balance, and restraint prompted her to offer the following suggestion: "Before you leave the house, look in the mirror, and remove one accessory."⁵

As our world becomes increasingly complicated and fast, as we attempt to navigate the racing complexity and the ever-accumulating clutter of our lives, a modest commitment to recalling the power of simplicity seems key right now. To this end, Chanel's fashion tip has always struck me as a metaphorical reminder of how crucial it is to be

---

3. Ibid.
4. Alice MacKrell, *Art and Fashion* (New York: Sterling Publishing, 2005).
5. "The most inspiring Coco Chanel quotes to live by," *Vogue*, August 16, 2018, www.vogue.com.au/fashion/news/the-most-inspiring-coco-chanel-quotes-to-live-by/image-gallery/b1cb17be7e20734d0b255fbd5a478ed4.

intentional, regular, and purposeful about paring down, cutting out, and removing the extraneous that distracts from the whole.

What if we considered removing one thing, just one task or item that we might think is required of us, from our plates? Take a look at your to-do list for today or perhaps for this week. Think about what could be dropped altogether. Maybe say "no" to something. Not everything is vital. Not all is needed. And in the tug-of-war of life, sometimes we ought to tug in the direction of less, not more.

Take a look at yourself. What are you carrying? What have you taken on? What if you set something down? Something that's not truly requisite, not really complimenting the look, the feel, the overall purpose of your life? Might a strategic excision improve things, simplify matters, and provide you a new outlook, fresh clarity, and the time required to be present to what is truly important?

More indispensable than any article of clothing you own, more crucial than anything you possess, is your time. Don't overload your day. Remove something. Create space for yourself to think, to meditate, to pray. Don't over-accessorize your attention. You'll look better. You'll feel better. Translate Chanel's fashion tip beyond the realm of the runway. Think of the integrity of the whole and subtract what distracts. Before you leave the house, check the mirror, think about what's ahead, and remove one thing.

God, help me today to simplify, harmonize, and pare back the "too much." Amen.

13

Two Lenses

> *. . . the compound of the two produces an undistorted picture.*
> —Eric Weinstein

Recently I listened to a dialogue between two formidably intelligent atheists—one a neuroscientist, author, and podcaster, the other a New Testament scholar and university professor who, somewhere in his twenties, had lost his faith.[1] They conversed in a generally respectful way about Christianity, but occasionally the guest couldn't help chuckling about what he now saw as the naïveté of his youth and his now-abandoned beliefs. Likewise, though the host explored the claims of Christianity with an honest desire to understand, his tone too, at times, belied a dismissive incredulity. At certain moments, listening to the back and forth, I could almost feel them both shaking their heads at what they considered the folly of religion.

While sometimes it's hard to engage with such programs because the claims of Christianity are often straw-manned or just labeled as foolishness, because both men were clearly smart, knew their Scripture well, and exhibited an authentic sense of curiosity about their subject and its ramifications with regard to how one lives, I listened to the whole thing, finding it both interesting and intellectually challenging.

---

1. Sam Harris, host, *Making Sense Podcast*, Episode 125: "What Is Christianity?: A Conversation with Bart Ehrman," May 1, 2018, www.samharris.org/podcasts/making-sense-episodes/what-is-christianity.

As the podcast ended, my mind went quickly to another interview this podcaster had done with a brilliant mathematician during which the mathematician revealed that though he was deeply committed to science and reason, he also took his Jewish roots and faith seriously. "I'm fond," the mathematician said, "of the metaphor of the double distortion—of somebody wearing glasses. Their eyes are distorted and the glasses further distort them, but the compound of the two distortions produces an undistorted picture. There are ways," he continued, "in which I worry that the sort of new atheist project really has a very limited market, because it's very important for me, for example, on Friday night to go into a Jewish traditional dinner, where it's not 'wink, wink, nudge, nudge.' We actually go through it and try to do the prayers."[2]

The mathematician, a man named Eric Weinstein who holds a Harvard PhD in physics, humbly suggested to the host that all the centuries-old, crowd-sourced spiritual wisdom ancient believers utilized to survive and make sense of a baffling world shouldn't be so quickly discounted or contemptuously thrown away. There's a baby, he was saying, in what the host considered mere bathwater.

This seems to me to be the most compelling way to approach faith and doubt and life and all its mystery. Human beings have remarkable minds and an obligation to examine all that's before us with the precision lens of modern reason and cutting-edge science to focus our vision, but something else is in order too—the second lens. That is, when we also employ a spiritual lens—the lens of faith—laying it sometimes over, sometimes under the lens of reason in the right measure, the clearest possible picture of reality is offered to us as we continue our ongoing pursuit of truth.

I learned a new word not long ago. It's something we're all familiar with; we just didn't know it had a name. It's called a *phoropter*—that big piece of equipment eye doctors use to come up with the right prescription to correct our vision. You know the drill: the ophthalmologist brings the machine right up to your eyes and begins to

---

2. Sam Harris, host, *Making Sense Podcast*, Episode 41: "Faith in Reason: A Conversation with Eric R. Weinstein," August 1, 2016, www.samharris.org/podcasts/making-sense-episodes/faith-in-reason.

flip the lenses, switching them back and forth, asking you which is better, "one or two?" It's here that my anxiety kicks in. Sometimes—concerned that I might answer wrong when it's a close call and saddle myself with a bad set of glasses and poor vision—I want to say, "Both. Both are good."

Maybe that isn't such a bad answer sometimes. Both are good. Our sacred text, the Bible, is full of art, allegory, poetry, theatre, parable, and legend—all of which serves the truth. However, at the same time, not every recounted miracle is merely a metaphor. We shouldn't be so quick, even in a modern world, to quell all mystery or feel obliged to explain what's meant to be transcendent. Instead, as we make our way through the world, it seems wiser, humbler, and more, well, human, to embrace the tension the two lenses create and present—to allow the left and right brain to dialogue back and forth. To camp and decamp between the rational and the wondrous. To find a fluidity between the historic and the metaphysical. And to consider deeply both the visible and the invisible. Why? Because it's often at these junctions, using both lenses, that we find God, magnetized to truth, just waiting there for us to arrive.

God, as I try to sort it all out today with the two lenses, may I encounter you. Amen.

Focus

It's like driving at night in the fog. You can only see as far as your headlights, but you can make the whole trip that way.

—E. L. Doctorow

Not too long ago, my wife Kelly and I were in New York and caught a show on Broadway, an impressive staging of Shakespeare's *MacBeth*. While there are several striking lines in the play, one particular passage resonated with me. Early in the first act, after a victory in battle, the heroic MacBeth and his friend Banquo encounter three mysterious witches who foretell that MacBeth shall become "king hereafter." And right there, the tragic flywheel of MacBeth's ambition begins to spin, leading eventually to his ruin. But the words that stuck with me most in the scene were not those of MacBeth but of Banquo, who also sought a prediction from the soothsaying women—one about himself. "If you can look into the seeds of time," he urges, "and say which grain will grow and which will not, speak then to me . . . ."[1]

We all have our issues with the murkiness of the future. When I'm watching a sporting event, if the score's tight, every few minutes I check the ESPN app on my phone, clicking on their Gamecast function. I then scroll down to a feature called "Win Probability," which reveals the percentage likelihood that one team will win and the

---

1. William Shakespeare, *MacBeth*, The Complete Works: The Edition of the Shakespeare Head Press (New York: Dorset Press, 1988), Act 1, Scene 3.

other lose based on what's occurring out on the field at that particular moment. Given that the outcome of the contest is clearly not within my control, it's hard to say why I do this. I guess I'm just seeking arithmetical evidence to support my hope that my team might be able to come back if they're behind or—if my team is ahead—reassurance that they're likely to hold on to their lead. Not content to just let things play out, I lean into the future, seeking some sort of illusory control over the game's outcome.

We all want more information to bring to bear to what might be over the horizon. But here's the thing—whether we employ high-tech quantitative analyses and mathematical algorithms or quixotic consultations with self-proclaimed psychics—the future will always remain shrouded in mystery. And, if we want to maintain a decent quality of life, we have to be at peace with this.

The late novelist E. L. Doctorow was once asked in an interview about how he plotted out the stories in his intricate novels. He told his interviewer this: "It's like driving at night in the fog. You can only see as far as your headlights. But you can make the whole trip that way."[2] While Doctorow's comments were about the process of writing, they ring true in a more expansive way as well. Our whole lives transpire within this sort of fog; the further we try to look ahead, the blurrier it gets. However, despite this fog, despite the uncertainty, despite our inability to see ahead, Doctorow is telling us that things have a way of revealing themselves to us when needed if we're able to remain closely attuned to where we are.

Think for a minute about the last time you were driving late in the evening down a dark road blanketed in a thick mist. Consider the level of concentration you brought to the task. How you slowed down to attend everything emerging from the hazy darkness ahead. How you held the wheel, calibrated your steering, and focused with your full attention on what was within your limited control based on what you could see.

My point isn't that we have to white-knuckle our way through life or that we ought not think or plan ahead; I simply want to put a

---

2. George Plimpton, *Writers at Work: The Paris Review Interviews*, 2nd series (New York: Viking Press, 1963).

few questions before us. What if we narrowed down our time horizon a little? What if we focused our awareness on the present sequence of visible moments and events—the things right in front of us—attending to them as they arise? What if we tried to lean more deeply into the notion that it's not beyond us to make the whole trip like this? What if we more closely embraced the present moment—today, this very day—trusting that things will be disclosed as needed? And what if, counting on both the hope and the reassurance our faith gives us, we relied on the notion that our God is with us always, even in the fog?

God, may I live in the moment, focused—present to the things before me today—making the whole trip relying on you. Amen.

The Law of the Gift

I don't know what your destiny will be, but one thing I know: the ones among you who will be really happy are those who have sought and found how to serve.
—Albert Schweitzer, 1875–1965

Albert Schweitzer is one of those historic figures who accomplished so much, it was as if he lived multiple lives at once. An influential theologian, he wrote books on the historicity of Jesus and the mysticism of St. Paul.[1] A skilled organist, he invented innovative recording techniques and devoted himself to the rescue and restoration of historic pipe organs all over Europe.[2] As a musicologist, he was one of the world's foremost experts on the compositions of Bach.[3] As a philosopher, he won the 1952 Nobel Peace Prize for his book *Civilization & Ethics*, which set out a philosophical idea he called, "Reverence for Life."[4] Still, even with this long list of achieve-

---

1. Albert Schweitzer, *The Quest of the Historical Jesus* (New York: Macmillan, 1910); and *The Mysticism of Paul the Apostle* (Baltimore: Johns Hopkins University Press, 1931).
2. "Albert Schweitzer and His Hospital in Africa," *SciHi Blog*, Daily Blog on Science, Tech & Art in History, March 21, 2021, scihi.org/albert-schweitzer-hospital-africa/.
3. G. Seaver, *Albert Schweitzer: The Man and His Mind* (London: A. & C. Black, 1951).
4. Gunnar Jahn (chairman of the Nobel Committee), Award ceremony speech for Albert Schweitzer, Nobel Peace Prize 1952, 10 December 1953, www.nobelprize.org/prizes/peace/1952/ceremony-speech/.

ments, most of us know Schweitzer not as a musician, a philosopher, or a religious writer but as a medical doctor who founded a landmark hospital in Africa.

In 1912, with funds raised mostly through his own concerts and barely enough equipment to run a small clinic, he set out with his wife, Helene, down the Ogooué River in what is now the nation of Gabon in Africa to establish a medical practice.[5] Albert and Helene saw more than two thousand patients in 1913, some of whom traveled many days and hundreds of miles to get there. The ministry grew, and soon the Albert Schweitzer Hospital was built. Though Schweitzer considered his work as a medical missionary responsive to Christ's call to spread the gospel, he also viewed his healing labors as a miniscule recompense for the damage wrought during the long era of European colonization of Africa. Operating the hospital for decades through both World Wars, in his later years Schweitzer then took up the causes of ecology and peace, advocating against the proliferation of nuclear weapons with luminaries such as Albert Einstein.[6] He also continued to write, to see patients, and to nimbly play the organ until, in 1965 at age ninety, he died in Africa. Schweitzer is buried not far from the hospital he founded, his grave on the banks of the Ogooué River, marked only by a modest cross he fashioned himself.[7]

Years before, in a 1935 speech in Wakefield, England, Schweitzer said to a group of young students, "I don't know what your destiny will be, but one thing I know: the ones among you who will be really happy are those who have sought and found how to serve."[8]

Certainly, the Ten Commandments and the other rules for living are gifts from God that show us how to lead good, well-ordered,

---

5. Howard Markel, "Dr. Albert Schweitzer, a renowned medical missionary with a complicated history," *NPR*, January 14, 2016, www.pbs.org/newshour/health/dr-albert-schweitzer-a-renowned-medical-missionary-with-a-complicated-history.

6. Albert Schweitzer, "Nobel Lecture," *The Nobel Prize*, November 4, 1954, www.nobelprize.org/prizes/peace/1952/schweitzer/lecture/.

7. See the image at en.wikipedia.org/wiki/Albert_Schweitzer#/media/File:Robert_Brumter_-_Gabon_31.jpg.

8. Steve Perisho, "Schweitzer on Service," *Liber Locorum Communium*, October 25, 2010, citing a scan of the address supplied by Louise Leach, administrative assistant to the Silcoates School Foundation.

ethical lives. We might call these blessings of divine instruction the *Gift of the Law*. However, God gives us something else as well. Something just as important.

Just as God provided the *Gift of the Law*—rules for us to follow—God has also set deeply into our moral conscience something we might call the *Law of the Gift*. Jesus expressed the essence of the *Law of the Gift* when he said that in clinging to our lives too tightly, we lose them, but when we learn to give them away, we find them. And though this seems something of a paradox, it too is a law—a natural law, a thing of nature. It's not changing. It's embedded in our humanity, in our operating system as a decisive force. It tells us this: self-giving, not self-assertion, is the path to human flourishing.

God has put within our grasp how we feel at the end of each day. It seems to be written indelibly on our hearts that if we put in a good day's work, volunteering ourselves from a place of choice and free will to help and humbly serve others in some way, we can reliably feel in some measure a sense of wholeness, a sense of peace, and a sense of happiness within ourselves when the day ends.

> *"I don't know what your destiny will be, but one thing I know: the ones among you who will be really happy are those who have sought and found how to serve."* God, help me today to reorder my life around the Law of the Gift. Amen.

Agency

We can't guarantee success . . . but we can do something better. We can deserve it.
—John Adams, letter to Abigail Adams during the Revolutionary War

David McCullough is a national treasure. His presidential biographies about John Adams and Harry Truman both won Pulitzer Prizes. His more recent book about the Wright Brothers is winsome and marvelous, and his compelling, story-driven accounts of the construction of the Panama Canal (*The Path Between the Seas*, 1978) and the Brooklyn Bridge (*The Great Bridge*, 1983) are fascinating page-turners. McCullough has a remarkable speaking voice too. He narrated Ken Burns's acclaimed Civil War series, several episodes of PBS's *The American Experience*, and a number of other television shows, including award-winning documentaries about the Statue of Liberty, the Donner Party, and the D-Day invasion. Whether narrating, giving viral commencement speeches, or in his own brilliant writing, McCullough seems unswervingly drawn to projects and stories that uncover the unique combination of grit and pluck found historically at the core of the American identity.

In his biography of Harry Truman, writing about the Berlin Airlift, McCullough paints a vivid picture of how America's steely determination and ability to improvise amid crisis coalesced in June 1948 when the Soviet Union blockaded all ingress and egress from the city of West Berlin. "We stay in Berlin, period," President

Truman said to his aides, and within two days, the United States and its allies, despite the obvious dangers involved in flying both day and night over hostile territory and a host of additional unknown hazards and escalatory risks, began shipping supplies to West Berlin by air.[1] At the height of the undertaking, a plane was landing every forty-five seconds at Berlin's airport.[2] The colossal effort would continue in earnest well into 1949 when Josef Stalin, surprised by the resolve of the Allies and embarrassed by his own nation's failure to prevail, finally called off the blockade. All told, American and British forces flew more than 250,000 sorties to the city, dropping fuel, food, and other essentials to save West Berlin as the Iron Curtain descended over the rest of Eastern Europe at the dawn of the Cold War.[3]

In a number of speeches, McCullough has cited the Berlin Crisis and the actions the United States took in response to it as an example of a hinge moment in history from which a higher, more philosophical lesson about life is placed on offer to us. McCullough puts it like this:

> And it seems to me that one of the truths about history that needs to be portrayed—needs to be made clear to a student or to a reader—is that nothing ever had to happen the way it happened. History could have gone off in any number of different directions in any number of different ways at any point along the way, just as your own life can. You never know. One thing leads to another. Nothing happens in a vacuum. Actions have consequences. These all sound self-evident. But they're not self-evident.[4]

McCullough's point is that we often view history and consider the past as being on a sort of preordained track that has led us inevitably

---

1. David McCullough, *Truman* (New York: Simon & Schuster, 1992).
2. Ibid.
3. Ibid.
4. David McCullough, "Knowing History and Knowing Who We Are," *Imprimis* 34/4 (April 2005), imprimis.hillsdale.edu/knowing-history-and-knowing-who-we-are/; transcript of remarks Mr. McCullough delivered on February 15, 2005, in Phoenix, AZ, at Hillsdale College National Leadership Seminar on the topic "American History and America's Future."

to where we are now, but when we fall prey to this kind of thinking, we fail to fully realize that it was because of actual human beings, behaving and acting through their own agency and under their own beliefs, that things turned out as they did. It was the will, faith, intelligence, and heroic actions of multitudes of great and good men and women who came before us, tirelessly contending with the forces arrayed against them in their day—many of which were wholly out of their control—that got us here. If we let this sink in, we might not only better comprehend the true measure our own good fortune but also better learn how to deploy our freedom and agency in the face of matters both in and out of our control.

In McCullough's extensive research for his biography of John Adams, he came upon a letter Adams wrote to his wife, Abigail, when the outcome of the American Revolution was most in doubt—that is, a moment in the course of history and in their personal lives when matters were terribly uncertain. Recognizing that while perhaps the ultimate outcome remained with Providence, Adams also pointed out what remained in their own hands. With characteristic American grit and pluck, Adams wrote this to his wife: "We can't guarantee success in this war, but we can do something better. We can deserve it."[5]

> *God, while perhaps there's no preordained track, I believe there is a preordained destination with you. May I discharge what is within my power today to deserve the good that you've providentially ordained. Amen.*

---

5. Ibid.

17

Legibility

... towering trees, sweeping slopes, splashing fountains, singing birds, beautiful statuary areas, and memorial architecture with interiors full of light and color.
—*Hubert Evans, describing his aspirations for his Forest Lawn cemeteries*

I like cemeteries, and there are some remarkable ones where I live in Houston, Texas. Glenwood in the Heights and Forest Park Woodlawn south of town are the most visually interesting. When I'm away from home in a city with a famous cemetery, I usually try to visit it. I recently spent time in Trinity Churchyard in Manhattan (where Alexander and Eliza Hamilton are buried), and I always feel edified after a visit to historic Arlington National Cemetery outside of Washington, DC.

The City of Angels, Los Angeles, has some fascinating cemeteries too. Just off Santa Monica Boulevard next to the Paramount Studio movie lot, shadowed by giant palms and dotted with manmade lakes, is a most eclectic one called the Hollywood Forever Cemetery. There, cinematic legends such as Cecil B. DeMille, Judy Garland, Tyrone Power, and Douglas Fairbanks are buried. Several more modern-day musical talents like John William Cummings (*aka* Johnny Ramone), Chris Cornell, and Scott Weiland are interred there too. Terry, the dog who played Toto in *The Wizard of Oz*, is memorialized at Hollywood Forever, as is Mel Blanc, who supplied the voice of Bugs Bunny and Porky Pig. On Blanc's grave marker, you'll find the words "That's

All Folks."[1] Throughout the sixty-two-acre property stand flashy statues and stones carved in the shapes of electric guitars, race cars, and dramatically weeping angels. They hold yoga sessions, midnight movie screenings, and concerts on the grounds, and the cemetery is also home to hundreds of cats that roam night and day. A large gaggle of ducks makes a pilgrimage to the gravestone of Douglas Colvin, *aka* Dee Dee Ramone, each afternoon as well. The style of the place is most often described as "Exotic Revival et al.," with the emphasis on the "et al.," as the cemetery has been run by a number of owners over the years without any devotion to a particular aesthetic or theme other than one I'd call "L.A. Camp." It's kind of cool, but really more odd than beautiful.

It's a far cry from the grounds of the Forest Lawn Memorial Park located not too far away in the Hollywood Hills. There are several Forest Lawn cemeteries in Southern California, all developed by Dr. Hubert Eaton, a metallurgist from Kansas City, who, when he purchased his first cemetery in Glendale, set out to change nothing less than how Californians viewed death.[2] A devout Christian, Eaton, in accordance with his faith, believed that we come into a realm of great joy after we die, yet when he looked around, he saw that most cemetery properties were "unsightly, depressing stone yards filled with inartistic symbols and depressing customs; places that do nothing for humanity."[3]

Taking a holistic approach to developing his land for the use and purpose he envisioned, he moved away from upright grave markers in favor of bronze plaques flush with the grass, then retained artists and architects to integrate the different sections of his acreage into a beautiful and harmonious space that visually reflected the hope he found within his faith. Forest Lawn, he made clear, would be composed of

---

1. See a photo at "Mel Blanc's Grave," *Atlas Obscura*, www.atlasobscura.com/places/mel-blanc-grave.
2. Adrian Glick Kudler, "Los Angeles is killing us: Finding the secrets of mortality at LA's most legendary cemeteries," Curbed Los Angeles, October 27, 2016, la.curbed.com/2016/10/27/13396168/los-angeles-cemetery-hollywood-forever-forest-lawn.
3. Hubert Eaton, "The Builder's Creed," Hubert L. Eaton—Forest Lawn, www.huberteaton.com/the-builders-creed.html.

"towering trees, sweeping slopes, splashing fountains, singing birds, beautiful statuary areas, and memorial architecture with interiors full of light and color."[4] And through painstaking and costly landscape design and thoughtful ongoing construction efforts, Easton's goal of producing an experience not of despair but of coherent beauty and resonant hope was realized.

When you take the fascinating walk around the Hollywood Forever Cemetery, you'll likely feel more like a tourist than anything else. At Forest Lawn, while it's still definitely LA, and you're likely to stumble upon some unusual graveside ceremonies and will no doubt encounter graves of celebrities as you look about, more than anything else, you'll find that Eaton's beautiful land is distinctly legible as a testimony to his faith. That is to say that whereas the style of Hollywood Forever is indeed "Exotic Revival et al.," a spiritual resonance emerges when one walks around Forest Lawn.

As we try to devote ourselves to living well-examined lives day by day and week by week—the kind of lives we hope will be well regarded, meaningful, and inspiring to others when they're recalled at a graveside or memorial service in the distant future—it might be a good practice to ask ourselves: How are our lives reading? Are they legible? Is there a coherence to them? Is there a sense of unity? Is there a distinct message emerging, or are we living out a sort of ad hoc, "et al." collection of experiences without any sort of overall theme?

Or perhaps consider this today: Even if it makes you feel a bit uncomfortable, go to a local cemetery, take a walk around, and briefly consider the notion of the legibility of your life.

Today, God, make my life more legible. Amen.

---

4. Greg Melville, "Inside the Disneyland of Graveyards," *Smithsonian Magazine*, September 29, 2022, www.smithsonianmag.com/history/inside-the-disneyland-of-graveyards-180980510/.

18

The Line

This line shifts. Inside us, it oscillates with the years.
—Aleksandr Solzhenitsyn

My son Charlie was an undersized offensive lineman in high school, but he used a good understanding of leverage and a high football IQ to contribute whenever he got into the game. On a basic running play, the general assignment of any offensive lineman is to push the defense back so his own team might advance the ball beyond the line of scrimmage. However, if the linemen don't do their jobs, or if they're simply overmatched by the other side, it's likely that the new line of scrimmage will end up behind rather than beyond the original line of scrimmage. Whenever Charlie lined up against a larger opponent—and he always did—you can imagine how hard his dad was pulling for him, believing in him, hoping for him, as he tried to move the line.

Aleksandr Solzhenitsyn was a commander in the Soviet army during World War II. Toward the end of the war, he was imprisoned for criticizing Josef Stalin privately in a letter to a friend.[1] Later, Solzhenitsyn wrote a Nobel Prize-winning three-volume narrative that recounted his years in prison and in exile. His book, *The Gulag Archipelago*, is filled with not only chilling accounts of his experience but also deep philosophical insights into human nature like this one:

---

1. Edward E. Ericso Jr., and Alexis Klimoff, *The Soul and Barbed Wire: An Introduction to Solzhenitsyn* (ISI Books, 2008).

> Gradually it was disclosed to me that the line separating good and evil passes not through states, nor between classes, nor between political parties either—but right through every human heart—and through all human hearts. This line shifts. Inside us, it oscillates with the years.[2]

Our own experience tells us that we are indeed alloyed like this, but just as Solzhenitsyn suggests, each of us has the moral capacity to shift the line, moving it forward, toward the good, and away from and beyond the evil that resides within the trenches of our hearts.

As I write this, the past few weeks our Jewish friends observed Rosh Hashanah and Yom Kippur. Rosh Hashanah is commonly described as the Jewish New Year, but I understand that it's more accurately thought of as a sacred day commemorating the birth of all God's creation.[3] Its liturgy is generally upbeat though it marks and then initiates a ten-day period of penitence, the Ten Days of Awe, as preparations are made for Yom Kippur, the Day of Atonement, the holiest of holy days. On Yom Kippur, observant Jews fast, reflecting on past mistakes, making amends with God and others, and seeking absolution for their sins and failures committed during the previous year.

Rabbi Meir Soloveichik is the rabbi of Congregation Shearith Israel in New York City. In a recent episode of the podcast *Call Me Back*, he compellingly explained the thought and history behind these Jewish holy days, suggesting that the spiritual notions of penitence, forgiveness, and grace are not just ideas for followers of Judaism but for all people universally.[4]

As he spoke, he acknowledged that repentance doesn't make a lot of sense. How, he asked, can we simply go to God year after year and say something like, "God, I failed and I deeply regret my failures. I'd like you to absolve my mistakes based on my sincere commitment

---

2. Aleksandr Solzhenitsyn, *The Gulag Archipelago* (repr., London: Vintage Classics, 2018).
3. Dan Senor, host, with guest Rabbi Meir Soloveichi, "Nidrei . . . misunderstood," *Call Me Back* podcast, September 30, 2022, episode 82 at 7:00.
4. Ibid.

to move forward."⁵ But then he pointed to the book of Jonah, the primary biblical text for Yom Kippur services, and summarized the story of Jonah and the Ninevites like this:

> Jonah is sent to the Assyrian city of Nineveh. Jonah doesn't want to go and originally we don't know why he doesn't want to go. And he comes to the city and says you're all going to be punished for your sins. (But then) they all repent and God changes his mind as it were and forgives them. Jonah says, "I knew this would happen. This isn't right. They did wrong and they deserved to be punished." But God says to him, "What do you want me to do—they regretted their sins, and I have mercy on them. I'm open to the human capacity to change and grow."⁶

When I consider the thoughts of Solzhenitsyn and Soloveichik in tandem, I'm left in awe. It's not only that God, knowing our frailty, seems to be fully on board with the idea of absolution and grace, believing deeply in our moral capacity to change, but also that this is God's ultimate project—the whole game. God knows the alloy that composes our hearts, and God must know we're overmatched sometimes. But God hopes for us and pulls for us. God knows we can advance. Our Father knows we can move the line.

God, may I feel your hope in me, sense your grace for me, and reorder my life today accordingly. Amen.

---

5. Ibid., at 22:45.
6. Ibid., at 23:15.

Furthermore, I Propose . . .

Furthermore, I propose that Carthage must be destroyed.
　　　　　　—*Cato the Elder, 234 BCE–149 BCE*

For a long time, the Roman senator known to history as Cato the Elder ended every speech he gave like this: "*Ceterum censeo Carthaginem esse delendam*—that is, 'Furthermore, I propose that Carthage must be destroyed.'"[1] It didn't matter what topic Cato's speech concerned; he would invariably conclude in this way before taking his seat. If the question at hand was about a mundane domestic matter—the harvest, an aqueduct, something about the disposal of trash in the city—he still ended his remarks with his emphatic position on the city of Carthage's existence.[2] It didn't matter what his audience had come to hear or the time allotted for him to speak; he always pivoted as he wrapped up in order to remind everyone that he considered it imperative that Carthage, Rome's rival city-state neighbor to the south across the Mediterranean, must not just be defeated but be altogether obliterated.

Although Rome had already been victorious over Carthage in what historians call the First and Second Punic Wars—in Cato's time—the Carthaginians, from their bustling seaport city located along on the northern coast of present-day Tunisia, continued to vex the Romans, inflicting losses and ongoing humiliations on

---

1. In F. E. Adcock, "Delenda est Carthago," in *Cambridge Historical Journal* 8/3 (1946): 117–28.
2. Alan Astin, *Cato the Censor* (Oxford: Oxford University Press, 1978).

their bigger neighbor.³ Cato took note of this. A soldier himself, he had visited Carthage and, even after their defeats, saw that Rome's nemesis remained wealthy, angry, and altogether committed to plans to fight again. With this in mind, he considered Carthage an ongoing existential threat to his own country, and he said so. Repeatedly. It took up, we might say today, a lot of bandwidth in Cato's mind.

After Cato died, Rome did wage battle against Carthage again in what became known as the Third Punic War, and this time the Romans indeed razed their rival city to the ground, even salting the soil so that nothing would grow there in the future.⁴ The senate in Rome then passed a law stating that no structure could be built on their conquered territory in North Africa to ensure they would not have to address the matter again. Carthage had been destroyed.⁵

Marianne Thieme is a Dutch politician, author, and animal rights activist. For about two decades, she has led a political party in the Netherlands known as the Party for the Animals. Serving in the Dutch House of Representatives from 2006 to 2019, Thieme adopted Cato's ancient oratorical practice, only modified to some degree to suit her own political beliefs: *Voorts zijn wij van mening dat er een einde moet komen aan de bio-industrie*—that is, "Furthermore, we propose that factory farming has to be ended."⁶

While her formulation was perhaps not as dramatic as Cato's, Thieme, just like the Roman senator from whom she borrowed this phraseology, concluded every speech and address during her public career in this way. Just as Cato had done, no matter what the underlying subject, Thieme emphatically, repeatedly, and memorably expressed her deepest convictions—the key imperative on which her life's work was based—in this way.

---

3. See "Third Punic War," *Britannica*, www.britannica.com/event/Third-Punic-War.

4. Ronald Ridley, "To Be Taken with a Pinch of Salt: The Destruction of Carthage," *Classical Philology* 81/2 (1986).

5. Ibid., 140–46.

6. "Portret: Marianne Thieme (Partij voor de Dieren)," *NOS Nieuws*, May 28, 2010.

I don't know what you might think of these stated devotions of the Roman senator Cato or Marianne Thieme of the Netherlands, but what if, conceptually if not specifically, we considered doing the same thing as they did? That is, what if we were to adopt a *ceterum censeo* statement of our own—a "Furthermore, I propose . . ." declaration for ourselves?

Give it some deep consideration. What is imperative for you? What, more than anything else in the world, do you want to bring about in your lifetime or even beyond your lifetime? What would you propose? What sort of assertion is worth repeating again and again and again because it must, in your estimation, transpire? Can you devise an affirmation of your most closely held conviction in such emphatic language that no one, least of all you, might forget how you intend to spend the currency of your highest attentions and most effective energies? What noble endeavor merits such bandwidth in a life? What particular thing ought to be ordering your life more than any other? Think about it. Here, let me help:

Furthermore, I propose, _____.

God, help me to propose and then fix upon a single noble and well-considered aim for my life, exerting each day my primary though not exclusive efforts toward its accomplishment. Amen.

It All Accumulates

Compound interest always works in your best interest!
—Mr. Honest Money

A few years back, our church began offering a series of summer Sunday morning classes to our school-age kids—a variety of hour-long courses that touched on vital life skills, introducing them to different vocations and professions, and prompting their imaginations to explore such things further as they matured. There were meal-preparation demonstrations for those curious about cooking. Police cars and ambulances rolled into our parking lot, providing kids opportunities to speak with officers and paramedics about their work. There were lessons on architecture, music, sewing, and rocket science. I think we even had an astronaut on campus at one point.

As the church's little Sunday morning academy developed, my wife Kelly, a lawyer with an MBA from the University of Texas, was asked to prepare a course on money management. She went about preparing it, acutely aware of the draw of the other compelling courses being offered, and elected to spice up her offering by recruiting our teenaged son Hank to portray for her students a colorful yet rigorously ethical character with a nose for business named "Mr. Honest Money." As her class began, Kelly and Mr. Honest Money encouraged the kids to prudently pick and follow stocks, trade prized commodities like candy and Pokémon trading cards, and always remember the importance of giving from one's earnings.

However, even with Mr. Honest Money's dynamic personality, his sound financial advice, and the Pokémon cards, strangely his lessons remained less in demand than those of the chefs, the first responders, and the astronaut. Nonetheless, those who matriculated under Kelly's curriculum and Mr. Honest Money's prudent tutelage certainly learned some useful lessons. Chief among these being the power of compound interest.

"Compound interest," Mr. Honest Money suggested to the kids, "is like a bag of Halloween candy that makes more candy. And the new candy makes more candy too. And the new, new candy—well it makes more candy as well. It keeps going and going. *Compound* interest," Mr. Honest Money gleefully asserted, "always works in *your best interest*!"

And it does. Warren Buffet once said he owes his wealth to the good fortune of where he was born, his genetic makeup, and the power of compound interest. When Albert Einstein was asked what the most powerful force on earth was, he answered, "Compounding interest."[1]

The term refers to the interest an investor earns on his or her original investment—plus all the interest earned on the interest that's accumulated over time. For instance, say you've saved $1000 at age twenty-four, put it in a conservative mutual fund, and left it there, committing to contribute $150 every month to it whether the market is up or down, but averaging an 8.5 percent annual return. In forty years, as you approach a traditional retirement age, the funds contributed ($73,000) will have grown to $635,404. Enough for Mr. Honest Money himself to doff his tall green hat and exclaim to you, "Well done!"

And of course, as is often the case, what's true in one realm of life is true in others. In our educational endeavors, the ideas and notions we learn in a particular field build on one another. Connections are made between and among concepts, advancing us deeper into more

---

1. Jim Schlekser, "Why Einstein Considered Compound Interest the Most Powerful Force in the Universe," *Inc.*, January 21, 2020, www.inc.com/jim-schleckser/why-einstein-considered-compound-interest-most-powerful-force-in-universe.html.

innovative and sophisticated ways of thinking about a subject. Experience works like this too. The first time we do something, it's often difficult, but repeating an experience exponentially advances our understanding of the nature of the thing at hand as we build up an almost magical intuition about how to accomplish it more effectively.

Our relationships work like this as well. The more quality time we invest in a good relationship, the more value emerges from it. Finally, our connection with God is also the same. A friend once suggested to me that those who know God's Word the most seem to hear God's voice the best. The accumulated knowledge of Scripture tends to open our eyes and ears to what we ought to do when in a pinch. It all accumulates.

Unfortunately, something of the opposite is true too. Credit card debt accumulates quickly. Bad habits tend to accumulate and trap us. Unhealthy relationships seem to accumulate dysfunction. Wasting time seems to beget more wasted time. And neglecting our discipleship leads us further away from God. It all accumulates—one way or another.

With this in mind, we ought to take this lesson to the bank: each and every moment of our lives—each day, each week, each year—is crucial, not just in and of itself but in what it is accumulating.

God, may I accumulate wisely. Amen.

Wednesday

Growth

And God said, "Let the water under the sky be gathered in one place, and let dry ground appear...." Then God said, "Let the land produce vegetation: seed-bearing plants and trees on the land that bear fruit with seed in it, according to their various kinds."... And there was evening, and there was morning—the third day. (Genesis 1:9, 11, 13)

21

School

We have two lives . . . the life we learn with and the life we live after that.
—Iris Lemon in Bernard Malamud's *The Natural*

I was thirteen years old, attending middle school at Spring Branch Junior High, and had just gone to see the doctor for a checkup. The appointment went fine, but when my mother dropped me off at the front of the school, instead of going back in, I waved, she drove away, and I then wandered off, playing hooky for the rest of the day. I don't recall exactly what I did. I wasn't busted, but I didn't do anything of great import either. Ferris Bueller I was not.

Just after three o'clock, I crept back to campus where the buses were loading, quietly mixed in, boarded mine, and headed home without incident. It was only later that I started to feel guilty. Interestingly though, that little censorious ping I felt in my mind and heart didn't just emerge from the fact that I'd been truant and broken the rules, though that was definitely part of it. More palpable was that I'd been taught that I ought to put every moment to good use. There in my bedroom, it suddenly became clear to me that this was a rule of conscience that I sincerely believed was important. I truly wanted to live my life that way. So that evening, I resolved I'd never miss a class again unless it was for both a legitimate reason and a good purpose—and I never did. Now, before it seems that I'm holding myself up as a paragon of virtue, believe me, I'm not claiming to have always gleaned such lasting lessons from my past failures and transgressions, but I certainly did that time, and here's the thing: I think we're supposed to.

In Bernard Malamud's novel *The Natural*, and in the movie based on the book, gifted baseball player Roy Hobbs makes a youthful but life-altering mistake that takes his playing career far off track.[1] It's only when he's much older, his dazzling younger days a distant memory, that he finally makes it back to the place he believes his fate, his destiny, were always taking him. However, upon his arrival there, he faces yet another ethical dilemma, a crossroads at which his childhood girlfriend, Iris Lemon, the moral compass of the story, is present with him. And as Roy laments to her that he should have seen things more clearly long ago, avoiding his mistakes, Iris tells him, "I think we have two lives." The weary and now grizzled Roy looks up at her and says, "What? What's that?" Iris Lemon—whose first name implies the gift of vision, whose surname is suggestive of refreshment and light, and whose full name conveys that she sees things rightly through a lens of hope and optimism—turns to the regretful Roy to say, "We have two lives, Roy, the life we learn with and the life we live after that."[2]

Among the many lessons passed down to us in literature in general and in our sacred texts in particular, this concept of reclamation and redemption is undoubtedly one of the most salient and beautiful. In our Bible, other than the characters presented within the dramatic narrative as divine, most of the rest who wander onstage insist on making all manner of bone-headed moves, leading to every variety of catastrophe. Though we've all been shown the distressing results of their ancient errors and blunders, we seem intent on following in their troubled footsteps. However, in addition to this, our Scriptures, through story, poetry, parable, and law, also suggest that we have the capacity to change and learn from our mistakes. Cover to cover, God seems to call to us, telling us it's what we remarkable and rambunctious human beings are capable of when we see our

---

1. Bernard Malamud, *The Natural* (1952; repr., New York: Farrar, Straus and Giroux, 2003); *The Natural*, film, dir. Barry Levinson, Delphi II Productions, 1984.
2. Ibid.

lives with clarity and act with resolve. It's sort of our thing, God is saying—or it should be.

Life indeed is an educational process, a kind of school that we decide to play hooky from every so often. But it's also a school to which we can come back, returning to God, resolving with conviction to do better, and starting over. Consider making a new resolution to reframe your past, your regrets, and your failures as the life you have learned with, a preface to the life you're continually beginning anew, and a glimpse of the life you'll live hereafter.

> *God, today I thank you for both of my lives: the one I've learned with and the one I live with now. Help me continue to grow—to stay in school. Amen.*

22

The Dishes

Everyone wants to save the Earth; nobody wants to help Mom do the dishes.

—P. J. O'Rourke

Every so often, while preparing for what I hope will be a well-received lesson at church—perhaps a lesson about humility, patience, presence, or grace—something happens. In deep concentration, I'm briefly diverted by a call from someone with a minor need. Or perhaps while I'm writing, something arises in the office and I'm asked to lend help for just a moment. Or I'm at home, making good progress on an upcoming presentation, and I'm reminded about a household chore I've neglected. In such times, I'm sadly obliged to report, a huffy feeling often comes over me, accompanied by the self-serious thought that the mundane thing I'm now being asked to pitch in on is far less important than the crucial personal task I've had to set aside.

Certain endeavors we undertake offer us a higher degree of emotional satisfaction, salience, and personal validation than others, and we tend to triage this sort of work over the mundane, day-to-day little chores we're regularly called to do as a matter of course.

P. J. O'Rourke died in February 2022. He was both an acute observer of human nature and a uniquely gifted writer. As one of his eulogists, a journalist named Matt Labash expressed the subtext of most of O'Rourke's writing as this: "Aren't we all ridiculous?"

Typing out his remembrances after his friend's death, Labash decided to conduct an experiment. He had five of O'Rourke's twenty published books on his desk. "I am now," Labash wrote, "going to open each one randomly and relay to you whatever passage I see first."[1] Mind you, he said, this is not a greatest hits reel but a simple roll of the dice. Here's the first paragraph he turned to from O'Rourke's 1983 book *Modern Manners*:

> This brings us to a more drastic method of getting an audience: be one. Listen patiently while other people tell you about themselves. Maybe they'll return the favor. This is risky, however. By the time they get done talking about themselves and are ready to reciprocate, you may be dead from old age. Another danger is that if you listen long enough you may start attending to what's being said. You may start thinking about other people, even sympathizing with them. You may develop a true empathy for others, and this will turn you into such a human oddity that you will become a social outcast.[2]

Five random "dart throws" inside each of O'Rourke's five books produced an equally humorous, enchanting, or incisive passage. "Try this with any other writer," Labash wrote, "and see how quickly it fails."[3] And yet P. J. O'Rourke wasn't just a tremendous writer and a keen student of life with a particularly trenchant sense of humor; he was a remarkably kind human being as well.

Labash references a story relayed to him about a man named Sam Pocker who said that when he was seventeen, he went to a P. J. O'Rourke book signing. O'Rourke signed his book but noticed that Sam looked distressed and asked what was wrong. Sam said that, after years of being told he was a superb writer, his freshman writing professor had failed him. He'd just received an F on a creative writing assignment before heading over to the bookstore. O'Rourke asked

---

1. Matt Labash, "P. J. O'Rourke, 1947–2022, Brilliant writer, beautiful soul," *Slack Tide by Matt Labash*, February 17, 2022, mattlabash.substack.com/p/p-j-orourke-1947-2022.

2. Ibid.

3. Ibid.

to see the paper—a detailed four-page review of a dinner Sam had recently eaten at Kentucky Fried Chicken. Sam took the paper out of his backpack and stood there as this famous writer carefully read it through all the way. When he finished, O'Rourke looked up and said, "She's just jealous." Pocker grew up and became a published author himself.[4]

What if we have it backwards and all the little things, both singularly and also in their accumulation, matter much more than the big things? What if we valued being amid the audience more than being up front? Valued listening more than speaking? Became more attuned to what's going on inside the life of the person right in front of us than wrapped up in the self-centered, personal publicity tours our lives sometimes become? What if instead of being so enthralled with the big, we focused on the little, the local? What if instead of seeking the spotlight on the big stage, we just did our duty on a small one? What if we took up this notion as an area of growth we could lean into here in the middle of the week—here on Wednesday? What if instead of being so focused on trying to save the world today, we just helped Mom with the dishes.

God, you save the world. I'll do the dishes. Amen.

---

4. Ibid.

23

The Till

Never fail to attend in victory that which you would certainly address in defeat.

—*Jeff Van Gundy*

After my first year in law school, interested in the field of sports law, I took a summer job with the Texas Rangers baseball club. Though it was an unglamorous entry-level position during a losing season for the team, it gave me an opportunity to gain basic knowledge about the business side of sports. During the day I toiled in the box office selling tickets, and in the evenings I worked as an usher at the games. While I was a good usher—helping folks to their seats, answering questions about the stadium, and ensuring no one was injured by a foul ball—it wasn't long into summer that I discovered I was bad at selling tickets.

At the end of every day, when my supervisor reviewed the number of tickets I'd sold and counted the money I'd taken in, it always came out wrong. I'd either have given someone too much change or not enough change for their tickets. Another variation on this theme might involve having accidentally given a buyer an extra ticket or shorting a family a ticket at some point during the day. I don't think my supervisor suspected me of stealing or anything like that, but as the summer wore on, there was little doubt about my lack of skill at the ticket window. Consistently, either the team or one of its valued fans was shortchanged.

My ineptitude reached its zenith on a day that, to my surprise, the dollar total in my till and the number of tickets I sold matched for once. I felt the thrill of success. Finally, I was getting better at my job. However, these hopes were quickly dashed when, upon closer analysis, it was revealed that I'd managed to charge one customer for a ticket he had not received and, later in the day, given an extra ticket to a customer who had not paid for it. When I suggested to my supervisor that at least the number of tickets and dollars received lined up, she replied that I had no cause to feel good about this.

Jeff Van Gundy is a former NBA head coach and current basketball analyst for ESPN. He lives in Houston with his family and also serves on the board for a highly regarded, state-authorized charter school in Houston's Third Ward serving at-risk youth. Over the years, in listening to Van Gundy's post-game press conferences as a coach and his analysis during the NBA games, I've thought him a keen observer of human nature, a deep thinker with an exceptional mind. This view was reinforced in an interview he gave on a local radio show a few years ago. The subject of winning streaks arose, and Van Gundy asserted that winning often papers over what, in truth, might be poor performance. Winning hides things that losing readily reveals, he said, and went on to explain that there's only one way to avoid this trap of thinking you're doing better than you really are—and that's to honestly examine yourself without regard to external results. He then added philosophically, "Never fail to attend in victory that which you would certainly address in defeat."

The examination of our daily lives that our faith urges upon us directs us toward a regular review and reflection of what is going right, going well, and working out for us, but also to consider the possibility that even if the scoreboard might look the way we want right now, we still might be missing something important, something deeper about ourselves. We ought to consider the possibility that even though our till is coming up with the right amount each day, we might still be short-changing someone. Maybe even God.

I know an invitation to critically examine oneself is not always a big box office draw. It feels like agreeing to go to a game you know you're going to lose. But we can conduct self-examination in light of a faith that assures us God loves us and desires that we flourish. Approaching self-examination with this belief in mind should be a ticket we all want to buy.

God, today, lead me into an honest evaluation of myself so that I may grow and flourish. Amen.

Shaping Conscience

He played a great part in shaping my conscience.
                            —*Martin Luther King Jr.*

Michael King was born in 1899 in Stockbridge, Georgia.[1] Growing up, he developed an interest in preaching, practicing his homilies on his family's chickens. At age eighteen, boarding with the family of Reverend A. D. Williams—then the pastor of the Ebenezer Baptist Church in Atlanta—he became deeply impressed with how the Black church was fighting for racial equality in the 1920s. So impressed, Michael soon decided to become a minister himself. He'd also started to court Reverend Williams's impressive young daughter, Alberta, during that time, and in 1926 they married. It wasn't long before they had three children: daughter Willie Christine born in 1927; son Michael, Jr., in 1929; and the youngest, son Alfred, in 1930.

In 1934, now an up-and-coming pastor himself, Michael toured the Holy Land, then attended the World Baptist Alliance meeting in Berlin, Germany, as Hitler was continuing to consolidate his power in the Third Reich. While in Germany, Michael studied history and gained a deep appreciation for the Reformation figure Martin Luther's bold protests against the status quo, which had led to earth-shaking changes in the Old World in the mid-1500s. The experience

---

1. Unless otherwise noted, all information about King Sr. in this section is found at "King, Martin Luther, Sr., December 19, 1897 to November 11, 1984," *Stanford: The Martin Luther King, Jr. Research and Education Institute*, kinginstitute.stanford.edu/king-martin-luther-sr.

shaped his conscience so fundamentally that Michael changed his name to mirror that of the priest.

Upon returning from Europe, he also took to addressing his eldest son as "M. L.," though sometimes he just called him Martin. Young Martin remembered, after his dad's European trip, witnessing an encounter he had with a police officer who'd stopped the elder King for a traffic violation. When the officer referred to his father as "Boy," his dad responded by pointing to his son and asserting, "This is a boy. I'm a man, and until you call me one, I will not listen to you." The officer, shaken by the man's boldness, retreated. Just as the father's conscience was shaped by events and role models, now the son's was as well.

As he grew older, the younger M. L., though not encouraged by his dad to become a preacher, watched as his father became the leader at Ebenezer Baptist following the death of Reverend Williams. "My admiration for him," Martin said of his father, "was the great moving factor. He set forth a noble example . . . he played a great part in shaping my conscience."[2] Martin watched his father in the pulpit. He listened carefully to audiotapes of his dad too, studying his cadences and speaking style as the elder King continued to serve at Ebenezer for the next four decades. On one occasion, his father took his hand and left a shoe shop when they were asked to give up their seats. "I still remember," the younger King said, "walking down the street beside him as he muttered, 'I don't care how long I have to live with this system, I will never accept it.'"[3]

Having exerted such influence on the conscience of his son, thirty years after returning from Nazi Germany, Martin Luther King Sr. found himself not far from Berlin. He was in Oslo watching Martin Luther King Jr. accept the Nobel Peace Prize in 1964. "As M. L. stood receiving the Nobel Prize," he said, "tears just streamed down my face."[4] Later of course, sorrowful tears would fall in April 1968, when MLK was gunned down on a motel balcony in Memphis. Just

---

2. Clayborne Carson, ed., *The Autobiography of Martin Luther King, Jr.* (New York: Warner Books, 1998).

3. Ibid.

4. "King, Martin Luther, Sr."

a year later, the senior King would lose his younger son Alfred in a swimming pool accident, and then his wife Alberta was murdered in 1974 during Sunday services at Ebenezer Baptist as she was playing "The Lord's Prayer" on the church organ. He'd been the actual target.[5]

The lives of Martin Luther King Sr. and his son show us that there's a peculiar confluence of experience and agency, of events and decisions, of beauty and tragedy that plays out mysteriously throughout the course of human life. Our consciences are often crafted by moments in time when a unique person, a wonderful or terrible event, or the content of a compelling book or teaching resonates so powerfully inside our souls that it exerts a distinct gravitational pull upon us. But we also have agency in shaping our consciences. We choose whom we will let influence us.

In honoring Martin Luther King Jr., our country has chosen to let what influenced him influence us—the Sermon on the Mount, the nonviolent resistance writings and courageous actions of Mohandas Gandhi in India, the mentorship and friendships of other civil rights leaders like Benjamin Mays and Bayard Ruskin. But what influenced him most of all, it appears, was what he saw in his remarkable father.

Father God, today, shape my conscience. Amen.

---

5. Rebecca Burns, "The Murder of Alberta King," *Atlanta Magazine*, June 28, 2012.

Trying Enough Cases

If you're winning all your cases, you're probably not trying enough cases.

—*Weldon Funderburk*

I began practicing law just as my dad, Weldon Funderburk, began the process of retiring from his work as a litigator, but he was a great source of advice while I slowly gained my footing as a young lawyer. He'd offer me little nuggets like this one: "It's easy to be bullish about somebody else's case." That is, if you're not the one whose name is on the pleadings and who has to answer to the client, often you fail to appreciate all the warts and weak spots of a given matter. Only when it's your responsibility to make the final call in a legal dispute do you begin to see the whole situation soberly and with clarity.

Another of his lessons went like this: "The lawyers on the other side are probably just as worried about their case as you are about yours." This conveyed to me that just about every argument has holes in it, and it behooves us to critically and strategically assess the weaknesses our opponent is facing rather than becoming fixed on our own.

Finally, perhaps the best professional advice he ever gave me went something like this: "If you're winning all your cases, you're probably not trying enough cases." While this guidance was in the narrower context of practicing law, as I've gotten older and changed professions, I've recognized that what he was saying applies to more broadly to life, and it was probably meant to all along. We shouldn't live always afraid of losing. We ought not be obsessed with a perfect record. We can't live a full and worthy life when focused on eliminating or avoiding every possible mistake or potential pitfall. We're going to make some errors. We have to acknowledge this because living with constant fear of loss is, in the end, worse than merely losing. It's embarrassing to crash and burn in front of people. But while it takes a toll on our self-esteem to lose, so does failing to enter the fray at all. A life of timidity is not what God has called us to and not a terribly interesting or compelling way to live our days anyway.

While most of the wisdom I received during my law career was from my father, whenever I found myself in the middle of the challenge and difficulty of a jury trial, my mind invariably turned to a book of counsel my mother gave me when I graduated from law school—a collection of Scripture arranged such that I could find the right verse for almost any need at hand. When I required courage, anxious that I might stumble, lose, or fail, I'd always search for the advice Paul offered to Timothy back in the first century. He wrote his young protégé these words in the short volume we now call 2 Timothy: "For God has not given us a spirit of timidity, but of power and love and sound mind" (2 Tim 1:7).

I don't know what you have in front of you over the next few days, weeks, or the rest of this year, but if you're living within the spirit of this passage, recognize that some failure will and probably should be a part of it. Read Paul's words to Timothy again and let them quell your anxiety. Read them again if you're burdened by the fear of not always excelling. And read them again if you're considering trying something new and difficult or beginning a new season of your life. Now read them one more time as you internalize the notion that failure is a crucial part of the alloy that composes our existence. It's part of living a good and rigorous life. If you're winning all your cases, you're probably not trying enough cases.

Whatever is ahead for you this week, approach it not with a spirit of dread or fear or timidity but with the power of Christ in hand, the love of God in your heart, and the sound and sober mind bestowed upon you by the Holy Spirit.

God, as this week progresses, may I learn to live more boldly without the fear of failing. Amen.

26

Healing

Notice how the cross and the doors and the clock are all off-center, yet it still remains in balance.
—Columbus, *2017*

Rcently I had breakfast with a couple of old friends. While I wouldn't go as far as to say our conversation was *dominated* by detailed discussions about our respective medical conditions, let's just say the topic arose more than once. It started to remind me of those commercials warning us about turning into our parents. It's inevitable, I guess.

Having shared this, I think I've become pretty philosophical about the process of getting older. First of all, it's happening whether I like it or not. That's the way it works. But I pushed back against it for a long time. As I moved into my early forties, I took it poorly when it became undeniable that I wasn't as fast or as strong or as durable as I used to be. Then I experienced an event that left me with double vision in one of my eyes. I remember sitting in an office asking a surgeon, "So you're saying I just have to live with it?" He responded that there was nothing to be done, but that as my brain compensated for it, I'd get used to it. And even if I didn't, I would still have to. Physically, it couldn't be healed.

We each collect a series of indelible scars—both physical and psychological—as our lives proceed. They organically arise from the troubles we encounter, the maladies we contract, the injuries we sustain. Then time itself leaves permanent marks on our bodies: ossified bones, weakened muscles, forgetful minds, poisoned organs.

Then there are our spirits. They encounter blows as well. Some sorrows we don't ever fully overcome. There are losses that stick, experiences that, in ways both seen and unseen, take a bite out of us, fractionalizing us and diminishing us in a manner that brooks no pharmaceutical answer. No biological resolution. No medical cure. There are simply things that happen to us from which we can never be fully healed.

However . . .

I was at Houston's Methodist Hospital this past week, and it struck me anew that though their mission focuses on healing our physical afflictions and frailties, they're quite overt about the crucial importance of tending the human spirit as well. It's telegraphed in the vibrant yet soothing paintings adorning the hallways. It's in the vivid photo galleries, the quiet gardens, and the sacred chapels nestled here and there around and between the buildings. It's in the form of the striking statue of Christ in the main lobby and a sprawling mosaic mural depicting him with hands outstretched on a wall above the hospital's main surgical waiting room. It's in the live music coming from the piano and pianist near the front entrance and in the singers preparing to perform in a nearby atrium along with a string quartet. With Scripture etched in stone around the campus and uplifting poems—Dickinson, Frost, others—arrayed across the elevator banks, it's clear that those stewarding the hospital space have more than physical healing in mind.

Our healing comes in many forms. Even if it's only a measure of healing, even if it's only temporary healing targeted toward conditions that are intractable, even incurable still placed on offer to us. Perhaps we don't as readily think of things like poetry, music, paintings, and sculpture as healing because they're not completely curing. But neither, in the end, is medicine.

I recently rewatched a beguiling, evocative movie called *Columbus* that suggests there's a healing power even in architecture. "You see," one character says to another as they ascend the steps of a church, "how the door, the cross, and the clock are all off-center, yet it still remains in balance."[1] The characters go on to speak of religion and modernity and finding harmony. Healing harmony.

Where might you find such harmony? What is *your* healing? What is the thing that heals you? Even if it's only temporary. Even if it's only partial. It might come in an unlikely place, in an unexpected form. Pitching batting practice to my sons' baseball teams always left me exhausted yet cleared of my own stingy pathologies. Churchill found calm in painting landscapes. It staved off "the black dog," as he called his psychic pain. What is it for you? Maybe it's fishing. Sweating it out in a yoga studio. A meditative walk that clears your mind. Listening to your soul as you listen to music. Maybe you have a favorite building. Approach it this week again in thought. Go to a museum today. Choose a single painting and gaze at it for half an hour. Or just have breakfast with some old friends and witness a healing grace unfold.

God, today, may I find the time, and my place, to heal. Amen.

---

1. *Columbus*, directed by Kogonada, produced by Andrew Miano, Aaron Boyd, Danielle Renfrew Behrens et al., 2017.

Botherations

I had botherations that led to good things.
—Shelby Foote

"I can't begin to tell you the things I discovered while I was looking for something else," Shelby Foote once told a magazine writer.[1] While researching and writing about one Civil War battle, one general, or one politician, a vague recollection of some fact, a quote, or an obscure anecdote he'd read in the past would creep into his mind. Frustrated that he couldn't remember it or where to find it, he'd further focus his thoughts. He explained it this way to his interviewer: "By golly, there's something [General Grant's Chief of Staff] John Rawlins said at that time that's real important. *Where did I see it?* Then I'd remember it was in a book with a red cover, close to the middle of the book, on the right-hand side and one third from the top of the page."[2]

With this, Foote would put down the inky dip pen he used to draft all his manuscripts, arise from his desk, and head over to his bookshelf in search of the elusive fact he had in mind. "I'd spend an hour combing through all my red-bound books. I'd find it eventually, but *I'd also find a great many other things in the course of the search.*"[3]

---

1. "Shelby Foote, The Art of Fiction, No. 158," interview by Carter Coleman, Donald Faulkner, and William Kennedy, *Paris Review* 151 (Summer 1999), www.theparisreview.org/interviews/931/the-art-of-fiction-no-158-shelby-foote.
2. Ibid.
3. Ibid.

Foote succinctly summed up these bonus discoveries he had made: "I had botherations that led to good things."[4]

I was in high school and had just gotten my driver's license near the beginning of the summer. I was driving with a friend to play racquetball one morning when we were diverted by some construction. Detoured, we headed down an alternate street we hadn't planned to be on when we saw something quite curious ahead—a girl walking a goat. We slowed down to see the goat and discovered as we got closer that we knew this young woman walking it. She went to our high school. Her name was Kelly, and while Kelly and I were already more than acquaintances, we weren't close friends. We waved to each other, then I pulled the car to the side of the road so we could talk to her. Upon closer inspection, it turned out it wasn't a goat she was walking but a dog. Her boxer Gus had just gotten his ears fixed at the vet, so they were taped with stiff white bandages and standing up rigidly; they looked just like goat horns from a distance. We spoke to Kelly and then, having managed to wrangle an invitation, my friend and I abandoned our plans to play racquetball and instead went over to her nearby house. We all ended up spending a good deal of time together that summer. Turns out, this girl with the goat later became my wife, and we now have two kids. (Human ones.) I guess it could be said that I've had some diversions, some *botherations*, that have led to good things too.

Our education, our careers, our daily work, our relationships seldom progress in a linear fashion. We get slowed down. We get knocked off course. We get diverted, shunted off the more direct, straight path along which we often feel we ought to be going. But here's the thing: more often than not, there's a deep and special richness to the diverted path. There's a unique, unpredictable, and unrepeatable quality to it—even a transcendent beauty sometimes.

Today and this week, as we seek to grow and to expand our souls as I think we are meant to do, what if we choose to meet these sorts of diversions, these *botherations*, these inevitable detours in our days not with frustration, irritability, or annoyance but with curiosity, equanimity, even a willingness to be beautifully blown off course? What if

---

4. Ibid.

we considered the possibility that the alternate, nonlinear, unplanned path might be better, richer, and more satisfying than what we originally planned or envisioned? Finally, what if we considered the sacred prospect that perhaps God might be calling us into these detours for an important, even holy, purpose.

Think about it. How many times have you been chasing one thing and in its pursuit found something far richer than what you'd originally set out to find? How many times have you been set and determined to go one way, but fate, destiny, or the spirit of God intervened and took you in another direction? Had it not occurred, maybe you'd have missed out on something truly wonderful. Thank God life can be like this.

God, indeed, thank you for our botherations and where they lead. Amen.

Baggage

Dad's bags aren't gonna make it!
　　　　　　　　　—The Darjeeling Limited, *2007*

Not long ago, our family packed our bags and went to Chicago. During a brief visit to the Chicago Art Institute, one particular exhibit made a deep impression on me. Oddly, it was housed in the basement of the museum. The Thorne Collection was commissioned in the 1930s by Narcissa Thorne, a Windy City heiress with a fondness for dollhouses.[1] Her collection is composed of a series of meticulously crafted, intricately detailed tiny rooms. Each miniature model, scaled at one inch to one foot, evokes a different age and place. Every miniscule chair and sofa is richly upholstered, each carpet finely designed. The little curtains are beautiful, the wallpaper ornate. There's even miniature artwork hung on the walls. Each mini room is masterfully lit as well, suggesting that the itty-bitty doors and teeny-tiny windows lead either into a little outside world or into another equally small adjoining room. With sixty-eight rooms in the exhibit, one leaves the museum's basement having, in some metaphorical sense, traveled both through time and all around the world. It's mesmerizing.

---

1. Charles Siebert, "Letter of Recommendation: The Thorne Miniature Rooms," *New York Times Magazine*, September 17, 2015. See also "Thorne Miniature Rooms," *Art Institute Chi*cago, www.artic.edu/highlights/12/thorne-miniature-rooms.

Two of the biggest fans of the Thorne Collection are famed film directors. When Orson Wells won his Oscar for *Citizen Kane*, he was asked about the innovations he made in lighting for his movie. He replied with a single word: "Thorne."[2]

Another director who cites the Thorne Collection as a major influence is Wes Anderson.[3] Viewing Anderson's films, one sees it immediately. The aura and ornamentation echoing the Thorne Collection is detectable everywhere—in the composition of every shot. It's in the natural, constant light, the eccentric elegance of the furniture, the charming handmade detail in every prop. Each costume accessory, every textiled wallpaper, the board games stacked in a closet, the perfume bottles arranged on a desk, the charming sofa pillows, the patterns in the carpet along the stairs, the wainscotting, the fixtures, the books on the bookshelves—all of it reflects the feel of the Thorne Collection. Anderson's whimsical yet melancholy, equal parts real and imaginary, diorama-like storybook aesthetic is reflected not only in the look of his films but also within the substance of his tales. "With the kind of stories I do—they tend to have some fable element, and I think my visual sort of predilections are somehow related to trying to make that tone and my writing work with performers, something like that," he explained.[4]

From the idiosyncratic cadences his quirky screenwriting requires of his characters to his unique "tiny room" aesthetic to the musical choices he makes for the most important scenes in his films, thinking of Anderson's movies as *fables* unlocks another layer of meaning in his art. And through this lens, the movie with which he delivers perhaps his most powerful fable-like truth is *The Darjeeling Limited* (2007), generally considered his most spiritual film.[5]

---

2. Meribah Knight, "Decking Out, in Miniature, for the Holidays," *New York Times*, October 9, 2010, www.nytimes.com/2010/10/10/us/10cncthorne.html

3. Ibid.

4. Wes Anderson, "'We Made a Pastiche' of Eastern Europe's Greatest Hits," *NPR: Fresh Air*, March 12, 2014, www.npr.org/2014/03/12/289423863/wes-anderson-we-made-a-pastiche-of-eastern-europes-greatest-hits.

5. *The Darjeeling Limited*, directed by Wes Anderson, produced by Wes Anderson, Scott Rudin et al., Fox Searchlight Pictures, 2007.

The Darjeeling Limited follows three estranged brothers—Peter, Francis, and Jack Whitman—each grieving, each flawed, each damaged (one physically, one relationally, one existentially)—as they take a spiritual journey, a train trip across the Indian sub-continent a year after their father's sudden death. The recurring gag and central metaphor of the movie is the image of the Whitman brothers hauling their dad's hand-crafted, cumbersome eleven-piece Louis Vuitton luggage set across the Indian countryside, through the train's narrow corridors, and into the foothills of the Himalayas where their mother now operates a Catholic convent. Their baggage hinders them all along the way.

Read like a fable, the luggage symbolizes the brothers' preoccupation with what they need not carry. They're constantly squabbling over their father's possessions—his prescription eyeglasses, his keys, his car—as well as the memory of his affections. Likewise, they become preoccupied by a series of other wholly unnecessary encumbrances they pick up along the way in India—an incredibly venomous snake, various pharmaceutical painkillers, shoes, a laminating machine, and their long-held grudges with one another until, in a beautifully filmed, brilliantly crafted climactic scene, Anderson poignantly delivers his fable's most useful moral truth. With The Kinks' 1970 song "Powerman" playing over the scene—the lyrics of which deal with discerning what we ought and ought not to pursue in life—the brothers, at long last, comprehend that their grudges and possessiveness are impeding their spiritual progress and literally shed their baggage, leaving it behind as they sprint to catch their departing train together.

I suspect that a quick clip of the fabled Wes Anderson's remarkable filmmaking might inspire you to let go of what you need not carry anymore.[6]

God, help me shed my unneeded baggage. Amen.

---

6. See "The Darjeeling Limited Ending," YouTube, www.youtube.com/watch?v=j9U216E-dTs.

If the World Were Perfect...

If the world were perfect, it wouldn't be.
—Yogi Berra

Lawrence Peter "Yogi" Berra quit school in eighth grade. At age eighteen, he enlisted in the Navy. Bored with training, he volunteered for a secret mission involving what he understood to be a rocket boat. "They asked for volunteers to go on a rocket boat," Yogi recalled later. "I didn't even know what a rocket boat was."[1]

Soon, part of a six-man crew on board what turned out to be a rocket-launching landing craft, Yogi found himself in the thick of the D-Day invasion, supporting troops and then landing on Utah Beach with his own crew. The following month, moving inland and into further combat in France, his unit was attacked by a German machine-gun nest in Marseilles, and Yogi was shot in the hand, but he didn't tell anyone because he "didn't want to scare his mother."[2] By the end of the World War II, in addition to later receiving a Purple Heart for his wounds in battle, he was also awarded a Distinguished Unit Citation and two additional stars for his service.[3]

---

1. Mark Lancaster, "Before Yankees career, Navy gunner Yogi Berra was part of D-Day invasion," *Sporting News*, September 23, 2015.
2. Jeremy P. Amick, "Baseball legend Yogi Berra experienced combat in U.S. Navy during WWII," *News Tribune*, October 7, 2019, www.newstribune.com/news/2019/oct/07/baseball-legend-yogi-berra-experienced-combat-us-n/.
3. Barry M. Bloom, "Yogi was military hero before a baseball star," *MLB*, September 23, 2015, www.mlb.com/news/yogi-berra-had-decorated-military-career-too/c-151195348.

Berra then began his storied baseball career, playing for the minor league Newark Bears until he was called up to the Yankees in 1946. He'd be in pinstripes for well over two decades. A fifteen-time all-star, he won the American League Most Valuable Player award three times, was part of ten world championship teams—more than any other major league player—and was elected to the Hall of Fame in 1972.[4] He is widely regarded as one of the greatest catchers in the game's history.

Despite his remarkable war record and baseball career, Yogi is now probably best remembered for what came to be called "Yogi-isms," perhaps the most famous of which was uttered while he managed the 1973 New York Mets. Asked late in the year if his team could come back from nine games down to win their division, he sagely pointed out, "It ain't over 'til it's over."[5] The Mets went on to win the pennant.

Everyone has a favorite Yogi-ism. Berra instructed younger players to pay attention in the dugout, insisting, "You can observe a lot by watching." Asked by a teammate why he never went to a particular pizzeria anymore, Yogi said, "Nobody goes there anymore. It's too crowded." Asked about games on the West Coast, he complained, "It gets late early out there." When a reporter queried him on why attendance was down, he responded, "If people don't want to come to the ballpark, no one's gonna stop them."[6]

Though Yogi told people, "I really didn't say everything I said,"[7] what's so great about his words is that if you spin around and squint a little, there's usually some profound wisdom on offer deep within them. "Always go to other people's funerals," he counseled. "Otherwise they won't go to yours."[8] When asked how he came up with

---

4. "Yogi Berra," *National Baseball Hall of Fame*, baseballhall.org/hall-of-famers/berra-yogi.

5. "Yogi-isms," *Yogi Berra Museum and Learning Center*, yogiberramuseum.org/about-yogi/yogisms/.

6. Nate Scott, "The 50 greatest Yogi Berra quotes," *USA Today*, March 28, 2019, ftw.usatoday.com/2019/03/the-50-greatest-yogi-berra-quotes.

7. Ibid.

8. Ibid.

a Yogi-ism, he confessed, "I don't make 'em up. I don't even know when I say it. They're the truth. And it is the truth. I don't know."

Other than his remark when he was told that the mayor of Dublin was Jewish and replied, "Only in America," my favorite Yogi-ism goes like this: "If the world were perfect, it wouldn't be."[9]

There are a few ways we can dissect this one after initially turning our heads in befuddlement. First, he's right—the world can't be perfect. It's impossible. Second, given human nature, it's probably the case that if everything in the world suddenly *became* perfect, we'd likely still find something wrong with it. Third, it's fair to say that "perfect" isn't always what it's cracked up to be. It doesn't always wear so well. Finally, embedded in Yogi's astute observation is an oblique but wise warning that pursuing the abstraction of perfection is a fool's errand anyway.

Oliver Burkeman is a British journalist who writes a blog intriguingly called *The Imperfectionist*. In it, he often urges his readers to stop chasing that imaginary moment we're convinced exists not too far away, when all our problems disappear, our trials and tribulations end, and our "real lives" can finally begin.[10] Such a place, Burkeman assures us, doesn't exist, and to believe that it does only delays our embrace of life and degrades our present experience. He advises us to get on with living, taking our imperfect world on its own terms, and doing what he calls "the next necessary thing" each day.[11] This seems like sound advice. Otherwise, we're merely inviting the disillusionment and frustration that repeated collisions with reality inevitably bring—"like déjà vu," as Yogi might say, "all over again."[12]

God of Grace and Growth, may I move forward with the next necessary thing today, refusing to fall prey to the idolatry of perfection. Amen.

---

9. Ibid.

10. Oliver Burkeman, "What if you never sort your life out?" www.oliverburkeman.com/never.

11. Burkeman, *Four Thousand Weeks: Time Management for Mere Mortals* (New York: Farrar, Straus and Giroux, 2021).

12. Scott, "50 greatest Yogi Berra quotes."

Wisdom

Because of low royalties, we can't reveal the artists.
Disclaimer, TEJ Records

I admit their television commercial had the sound and feel of a Ronco kitchen appliance sales pitch, but this company—TEJ Records—was offering something more: a double album chock full of terrific early 1970s billboard hits including "Bennie and the Jets," "Band on the Run," "Don't You Worry About a Thing," and "many, many more" per their persuasive spokesperson.

At the time, a 45 rpm vinyl single set a nine-year-old kid like me back about a dollar at K-Mart, but now these remarkably generous TEJ folks were offering me a compilation of two dozen catchy pop songs for only $6.99 total. On one hand, it seemed like a "can't miss" proposition. On the other, I had a more than fleeting suspicion that this might all be too good to be true. After weighing the matter closely, though, I tamped down my concerns and sent my money off to a PO Box located somewhere in Michigan despite my misgivings.

After a few weeks passed, sure enough the post office delivered a large double album-shaped envelope marked "TEJ Records— Do Not Bend," and with great excitement I retreated to my room. Careful not to bend, I began to tear open the big envelope as little by little, more and more of the distinctive orange and brown-striped album cover I'd seen on TV just a few weeks before revealed itself. I then delicately removed the first vinyl record from the sleeve and, holding it by the edges, settled it softly on the turntable of my little

Panasonic record player, prepared to enjoy the chart-topping voices of Elton John, Paul McCartney, Stevie Wonder, and "many, many more."

The opening piano chords of "Bennie and the Jets" sounded okay. But then Elton John started singing and I quickly detected something was off. It didn't sound like the real Elton John. There was something wrong with his pipes. Whoever was singing about Bennie and the Jets on this record was hitting the right notes, but there was something crucial missing. The voice lacked the same brand of distinctive energy, charm, and charisma I'd associated with the flashy bespectacled singer I listened to regularly on the radio. I remember experiencing a sinking feeling as I realized it wasn't Elton John singing at all. I lifted the needle and tried "Band on the Run." Same thing. Not Paul McCartney. I picked up the needle again and set it down on the Stevie Wonder track, but there was no wonder in Stevie's voice either.

I tried to listen to the record again, but a peculiar mixture of disappointment and outrage bubbled up inside me every time I did. I attempted to will myself to enjoy these counterfeit versions of the songs—to convince myself I'd not been ripped off by this TEJ Records outfit—but in the end, I could take no pleasure in any of it. The notes, the lyrics, the rhythms, and the tempos were all the same as in the originals, but none of them delivered anything near the emotional resonance, the soulful satisfaction, or the true joy of the real thing. Incensed that I'd willingly cooperated in the deception, I complained to my dad. Though sympathetic, he told me I'd learned a good life lesson: "You get what you pay for."

While right then and there, I vowed not to ever make such an error again, when I really consider it, I still make this same mistake all the time. I don't mean falling prey to commercially deceptive trade practices from shady record companies but willingly accepting mere facsimiles of what's real. I trade real connections for virtual ones. Instead of receiving the full power of an experience available to me if I were to give my undivided attention to it, instead I give something less to it, choosing to offer some of my attention simultaneously to a screen. And yes, while considerable inefficiencies are paid out in energy and time when we take the trouble of attending a meeting or an event in person rather than watching a close facsimile of it online, just as my dad said—we get what we pay for. If we want the real thing, there's almost always a cost to it. But the payoffs include intangible things of great value—the emotional resonance of awarding our full attention to another person, the soulful satisfaction of being physically present to a community, the feeling of true joy, the earned success of doing something the hard way rather than an easier way, and many, many more.

God, don't let me forget you get what you pay for. Amen.

Thursday

Awe

And God said, "Let there be lights in the vault of the sky to separate the day from the night, and let them serve as signs to mark sacred times, and days and years, and let them be lights in the vault of the sky to give light on earth . . . ." And there was evening and there was morning—the fourth day. (Genesis 1:14-15, 19)

Thursday

Do You Give the Horse Its Strength...

Do you give the horse its strength or clothe its neck with a flowing mane? (Job 39:19)

I'm sure there are others, but Angus Fletcher is the only person I've ever heard of who holds advanced degrees in both neuroscience and literature. He utilizes both deftly in his 2021 book, *Wonderworks: The Most Powerful Inventions in the History of Literature*.[1] Fletcher has taught at Stanford, worked with Disney/Pixar moviemakers, and now heads a thinktank at Ohio State that sorts out why particular stories affect us in the ways they do. In his book, he suggests that authors like Homer, Aesop, Dante, Shakespeare, Shelley, Austen, and Joyce were as much inventors as they were writers, deploying new "literary technologies" to generate an array of emotions that we need to feel if we are to flourish as human beings.[2] With innovations like irony, metaphor, rhyme, and inner dialogue, these authors and others are able to reliably conjure up feelings like consolation, gratitude, serenity, resilience, and joy—emotions that help us crack the code on love, loss, failure, and doubt and find the courage needed to pursue joy, hope, and lasting purpose in our lives.

---

1. Angus Fletcher, *Wonderworks: The Most Powerful Inventions in the History of Literature* (New York: Simon & Schuster, 2021).
2. Ibid., 13–28.

One such literary innovation Fletcher cites traces all the way back to the story of Job.[3] He points out that a rudimentary Job-like narrative had bounced around the Dead Sea Valley for centuries—the story of a good man who had lost everything yet held unswervingly to his faith and then received back all he'd lost. However, around 550 BC as the Babylonian exile ended, a Hebrew poet gave the story a rewrite. While the original version was designed to, as Fletcher puts it, "strengthen our neural commitment to justice" with the righteous man uplifted and our notions of fairness reinforced, this Jewish poet understood that something new was needed to make sense of what had happened to his people.[4] Something more nuanced and complex. So, in 1,000 new lines, he enlarged the story, one might say, to account for the actual experience of human life.

In the new version, Job, though still righteous, is more honest with God. "I cry unto Thee, O God," he says, "and thou dost not hear me: I stand up and thou regardest me not."[5] In response, God rebukes him, pointing out the vast difference between their stations in the universe: "Hast thou an arm like God? Or canst thou thunder with a voice like him?"[6] In this exchange, while part of us recognizes Job is on shaky ground questioning God, we nevertheless identify with him. This feeling is reinforced when Job apologizes: "I abhor myself and repent in dust and ashes."[7] This is all something new in literature—Fletcher calls it "an astounding neural leap."[8] Being placed sympathetically "inside the perpetrator's head," he asserts, produces something new and beautiful in literature; something that advanced our humanity; something we now call *empathy*.

When I consider how Job's story expands our souls, the remarkable life of Ruth Ann Brown comes to mind. Ruth Ann dealt with multiple sclerosis for more than thirty years, and I can't read Job anymore without thinking of her. Preparing for her memorial service

---

3. Ibid., 58–64.
4. Ibid., 57–58.
5. Job 30:20, KJV.
6. Job 40:9, KJV.
7. Job 42:6, KJV.
8. Fletcher, *Wonderworks*, 62.

last year, her husband Bill told me she loved the Disney movie *Secretariat*, the story of Penny Chenery, owner of the undersized, underdog horse that won the Triple Crown. Ruthie, as Bill called her, invariably teared up when the film started, and Diane Lane, playing Penny, began the story like this:

> More than three thousand years ago a man named Job complained to God about all his troubles and the Bible tells us that God answered. *"Do you give the horse its strength or clothe its neck with a flowing mane?* Do you make him leap like a locust, striking terror with his proud snorting? He pauses fiercely, rejoicing in his strength and charges into the fray. He laughs at fear, afraid of nothing. . . . In frenzied excitement he eats up the ground. He cannot stand still when the trumpet sounds."[9]

Why might this have brought tears to Ruth Ann's eyes? Was it the movie? The underdog story? Was it how God redeems our suffering? Or how Job's story generates empathy in us? Maybe it was just the happy defiance embedded in the words. It's so layered that it's difficult to sort out, but knowing the answer to the question—that it's not us but a sovereign God who gives the horse its strength and is also mindful of us—helps crack the code on love, loss, failure, and doubt and find the courage needed to pursue joy, hope, and lasting purpose in our lives.

I think that must have been it.

Awesome God, you alone give the horse its strength. Amen.

---

9. *Secretariat*, directed by Randall Wallace, produced by Mark Ciardi and Gordon Gray, Walt Disney Pictures, 2010. See also Job 39.

32

Ephemeral

Flowers grow without any literal meaning, they are just beautiful.
                                    —*George Balanchine*

Several years ago, I went to New Jersey on a business trip, then traveled back into New York City for the night, preparing to fly home the next day. With some time on my hands, as the sun went down over the city, I decided to go to the Lincoln Center for the Performing Arts because I'd never been before.

Located on the Upper West Side of Manhattan, the Lincoln Center is home to the New York Philharmonic, the Metropolitan Opera, and the New York City Ballet as well as the Juilliard School. Thus, on any particular evening, they might be presenting an opera there. Or a play. Or a symphony. Or a ballet. My plan was to get a ticket to whatever was happening that night.

I exited a yellow taxi under a winter-blue evening sky and took in the striking Gotham panorama all at once. The lights of Metropolitan Opera House at the center of the plaza glowed golden through the glass of its five soaring windows. The sound and motion of a beautiful water fountain in front transported me from the bustle of the Manhattan traffic yet still left me feeling as if I remained at the center of the world. I walked past the cascading water and into an expansive, breathtaking foyer. Symmetrically swirling, wide-curving staircases juxtaposed compellingly with the rectangular inlays of the large arched windows now behind me. Marc Chagall murals floated thrillingly on the walls like colorful clouds. A huge starburst crystalline chandelier hung above as lively theatregoers arrived decked out in stylish clothing.

The cavernous performance space evoked the awe of the European opera houses I'd seen in pictures, with rich woods, luxurious reds, and more starburst chandeliers hanging from the ceiling, yet the room also conveyed an intriguing American modernity with its sleekly tiered boxes scalloped five stories high. As I settled into my seat on the orchestra level, the chandeliers suddenly flashed with bursting light, then ascended magically away, announcing that tonight's performance was about to begin.

I was at the ballet.

I knew almost nothing about ballet and even less about George Balanchine, who choreographed this one. I was vaguely aware of his name, knowing only that he was—and this is my vernacular, not that of the elegant program I held in my hands—sort of the Babe Ruth of his art form, the twentieth century's most important choreographer. After emigrating from Russia in the 1930s, he founded the School of American Ballet and trained a generation of dancers to perform his prolific work.[1]

As the performance began, I found myself shaking my head in near disbelief at how the dancers had not only memorized their movements, positions, steps, and gestures but also executed them flawlessly, synchronized or complementing one another with both expression and precision. Without words, without voice, these athlete-artists were telling a story with only their motion, their costumes, and Balanchine's choreographic genius. While the story was soon over, even the story, in the end, was beside the point.

Balanchine himself thought telling a story, offering the audience a chance to find themselves in the ballet's plot or even to gather meaning from its narrative, was secondary to experiencing the beauty of it. He considered the fleeting nature of the performance central to how it conveyed this aesthetic. He often compared the ballet to flowers.

---

1. "George Balanchine," *New York City Ballet*, www.nycballet.com/discover/our-history/george-balanchine/.

"When you have a garden full of pretty flowers," Balanchine once said, "you don't demand of them, 'What do you mean? What is your significance?' . . . Flowers grow without any literal meaning, they are just beautiful . . . . A flower doesn't tell you a story. It's in itself a beautiful thing."[2]

We don't always fully appreciate beauty for its own sake. And we don't always comprehend the fortifying properties that even an ephemeral experience of such enchantment offers us. We readily allow what is unlovely in the world to draw strength, vitality, and inspiration from us, but beauty is restorative.

Beauty has the power to refill us. With a walk through a garden of flowers. In the sight of an illuminated bridge in the distance at night. Through the calming sound of tumbling water. In the way radiant architecture draws our eyes upward. In the melancholy glory of descending sunlight. In the charm of a delightful painting. In the appeal of stylish clothes. Or in the evanescence of ballet. Wherever you have the good fortune to encounter it, let beauty revitalize you, reenergize your capacity to love, and renew your aspirations to embody grace and beauty itself.

God, today, restore me with beauty. Amen.

---

2. Arlene Croce, "Balanchine Said: What was the source of the choreographer's celebrated utterances?" *New Yorker*, January 18, 2009, www.newyorker.com/magazine/2009/01/26/balanchine-said.

33

Unreservedly

Like it more unreservedly.

—*Christopher Nolan*

After finishing law school and coming home to Houston in my mid-twenties, I started attending church but did so in a tentative, reserved, and on-my-own-terms kind of way. About once, maybe twice a month, I'd arrive, and just as worship started, I'd find an empty pew near the back of the sanctuary. I'd follow along in the hymnal as everyone sang, maybe humming a bit during the refrains, then listen to the sermon somewhat engaged. As the service edged to a close, I'd check my watch as if I had somewhere else to be and quietly slip out the back. I might nod earnestly to an unavoidable usher or smile pleasantly at a congregant in my path, but my general strategy and overarching goal was to avoid all conversation that might lead to being cornered into some commitment I didn't want to take on. Having said this, I liked going. I liked being there. My arrangement worked out great—for me. It went on like this for several years.

Writing about one of our generation's most fascinating movie directors, Christopher Nolan, in *The Nolan Variations*, author Tom Shone recounts a series of dialogues he had with the director about Nolan's compelling films, including my favorite one, *Interstellar*.[1] While this remarkable movie can be categorized as a science fiction epic—a high-stakes rescue tale set deep in space that tackles complex scientific ideas like the nature of time and relativity—at its core, it's

---

1. Tom Shone, *The Nolan Variations* (New York: Knopf, 2020).

a cinematic hymn about the enduring bonds between a father and daughter, the remarkable human capacity for hope, and, most strikingly of all, the dimension-crossing, eternal power of love itself.[2]

In the chapter that focuses exclusively on *Interstellar*, titled "Emotion," Shone explains how Nolan evokes feelings of awe in the film with well-crafted shots, astonishing imagery, and an arresting musical score perfectly tailored to the movie and its themes. But then Shone turns a more critical eye on the film's intricately layered story, recounting the critics' complaints that there were holes in the plot and that Nolan had wrapped everything up a little too cleanly, a little too easily, a little too triumphantly at the end. As the conversation between author and director proceeds, Nolan, one can tell, becomes impatient with what he views as poorly grounded criticism, eventually telling Shone that people who really like the film don't see it this way.

"But I do like the film," Shone insists.

"Like it more unreservedly," Nolan replies.[3]

Sometimes I sense that God, with a graceful smile, might be saying the same thing to us: "Look at the imagery all around you. Its color and its glory. The stars above. The wonders to your left, to your right, and at your feet. Listen to the music that soundtracks your days—in the forest, at sea, in your symphony halls, and through your invisible airwaves. Consider the resonant artistry of the science that dictates how your world and the galaxies spin. Even with the unexpected twists and turns you might consider plot holes in the storyline of your lives, gaze at the whole before you. Yes, there are things to criticize—and some of your complaints are quite legitimate. There is suffering. Things don't always go according to the script. From the beginning this has been the case, but I am the great director and composer, even the great improvisor when this is required. And all shall end, if not so easily, triumphantly nevertheless."

---

2. *Interstellar*, directed by Christopher Nolan, produced by Emma Thomas, Christopher Nolan, and Lynda Obst, Paramount Pictures/Warner Bros. Pictures, 2014.

3. Shone, *Nolan Variations*.

Maybe it's counter to our natures to commit to anything without reservation—to arrive early, engage fully, and sing with abandon—but maybe we should try it. Maybe our desire to experience God on our own terms rather than on God's is exactly what holds us back. Maybe it's what keeps us from fully comprehending and embracing God's rescuing, enduring, dimension-crossing, eternal love for us and for all of Creation.

God, rid me of my faith's reservations and help me recognize all that you have placed before me today. Amen.

34

The Fullness of Reality

But every animal can only tap into a small fraction of reality's fullness.

—Ed Yong, An Immense World

Imagine that you've joined an elephant, a mouse, a robin, an owl, a bat, a snake, a spider, a mosquito, and a bee inside the confines of a cavernous high school gymnasium. Do you have the picture? There you are—each in your own way—exploring the space together. Now imagine the lights go out. This is how Pulitzer Prize-winning science writer Ed Yong opens his terrific book, *An Immense World*, which considers how animals experience the world so differently than we do.[1]

Back in the gym, the elephant, Yong writes, raises its trunk up high like a periscope sensing, feeling its way across the gym. The snake flicks its tongue to pick up scents and the body heat of the other creatures nearby. The antennae of the mosquito tremble and turn as it navigates through the air after catching wind of your breath and skin. When you swat at the mosquito, it startles the mouse, which squeaks at such a high frequency that the bat can hear it, but you and the elephant cannot.[2]

Yong continues to play out the scenario with the snake feeling the movements of the elephant via the vibrations of the floor. Meanwhile,

---

1. Ed Yong, *An Immense World: How Animal Senses Reveal the Hidden Realms Around Us* (New York: Random House, 2022).

2. Ibid., 3–5.

you hear the robin chirping next to you. Had the lights not gone out, you could no doubt see the red of the robin's breast, though the elephant can't—its eyes are restricted to yellows and blues. The buzzing bee can't see the red as you see it but experiences all sorts of colors well beyond your limited human vison. At the same time, the curved feathers around the owl's face are funneling the buzz of the bee's and mosquito's wings into its super-sensitive owl ears. It also hears the mouse scooting across the floor guided by its twitching mouse whiskers. The snake detects the mouse too, sensing its body heat coming closer. As the snake slithers toward the little mouse, the air is disturbed, making the snake's presence known to the spider, whose web acts as an extension of its own tiny body. Next, the bat, with its built-in sonar system, swoops downward from the rafters, locating the spider's exact position in its eight-legged dash across its gossamer web. Last of all, the red-breasted robin, sensing the hum of the Earth's magnetic field beneath the gym, pivots in a new direction and escapes through an open window, knowing somehow the climate is warmer to the south.[3]

With this marvelous opening, Yong demonstrates not only that each animal experiences reality differently from humans and from one another but also that each one is, in a sense just as we are, sealed up tightly "within its own unique sensory bubble," able to "tap into only a small fraction of reality's fullness." Along this theme, Yong continues chapter after dazzling chapter, exploring the hidden realms around us that we're unable to fully access. As he writes about ultraviolet light and the parts of the color spectrum we can't see, as he writes about scents and tastes, heat and pain, haptics and flow, echoes and electric fields, it becomes hard not to wonder what else might exist right in front of us that, due to our limited capacities, remains just outside the grasp of our perception and full understanding. What else might we be missing? More generally, what is this "fullness of reality" we and the other animals experience only a sliver of?

Thinking about these questions after reading a little more of Yong's book, I took a walk outside trying to focus on the many things around me I often fail to attend. There were birds singing at

---

3. Ibid.

all sorts of pitches from varying elevations and distances. Bugs were buzzing. Dogs were barking. There was an invisible breeze moving through the trees. Then also, there was my own breathing and an interior voice I recognize as mine operating inside the miracle we call consciousness within a medium we commonly call prayer. And from my narrow sliver of reality in this world, I knocked at the door to another hidden realm in pursuit of an encounter with the One who created the singing birds, the buzzing bugs, the barking dogs, the elephant, the mouse, the robin, the owl, the bat, the snake, the spider, the mosquito, the bee, the wind, the trees, the magnetic fields, and me. And I was left to conclude that all we experience and all that is before us that we can't quite yet know and can't quite grasp is *God*.

God, you are the fullness of reality. Amen.

Don't Look a Gift Universe in the Mouth

You should not look a gift universe in the mouth.
—G. K. Chesterton

When I took Spanish in high school, our teacher required us to translate a series of short Spanish sayings into English. The one that rolled off my tongue most readily went like this: *"Los lunes, ni las gallinas ponen."* It means "Nothing much gets done on Monday," but the literal translation is more colorful—"Not even chickens lay on Mondays." It came in handy later when our Spanish teacher decided to administer a pop quiz after a long weekend. *"Profesora, ni las gallinas,"* the class whined. *"Por favor, ni las gallinas."*

Another memorable one was *"A caballo regalado no se le mira el diente,"* which loosely translates to "Don't look a gift horse in the mouth." Literally, it means that if you happen to be offered a horse free and clear, you should take it. To check its teeth to verify its health or age reveals both a lack of appreciation for the gift and suspicion of the giver as well. The aphorism urges us to receive what is unearned magnanimously, gracefully, and as windfall rather than in a posture poised to complain about the gift's potential flaws and imperfections.

G. K. Chesterton (1874–1936) was quite a character. A prolific writer—memorable, quotable, irrepressible—he reveled in both the big and little joys of life. He said this, for instance, about his favorite brand of ink:

> I like the Cyclostyle ink; it is so *inky*. I do not think there's anyone who takes quite such a fierce pleasure in things being themselves as I do. The startling wetness of water excites and intoxicates me; the fierceness of fire, the steeliness of steel, the unutterable muddiness of mud . . .[1]

In this spirit, Chesterton penned nearly a hundred books, almost a thousand poems, thick volumes of short stories, and an untold number of essays. As a political philosopher, he developed thought-provoking concepts such as the one now known as Chesterton's Fence, which stands for the principle that changing customs and conventions should not be undertaken lightly or flippantly. When one encounters a fence out in an open field, there's wisdom, he suggested, in refraining from tearing it down until one knows why it was erected in the first place.[2] That is, before changing an existing rule or tradition, one should approach what's at hand with a dose of humility, considering fully the benefits of the status quo and the present circumstances. The rigor and depth of Chesterton's thinking is equally reflected in his prodigious writing on spiritual topics as well. No less than C. S. Lewis credited Chesterton's book *The Everlasting Man* as the treatise for "'baptising' his intellect" and setting the stage for Lewis's own conversion to Christianity.[3]

Chesterton, it seemed, always had the ability to penetrate to the heart of any subject he took up. Consider these pithy sayings as examples of his compelling way of putting things:

> Fairy tales do not tell children that dragons exist. Children already know that dragons exist. Fairy tales tell children that dragons can be killed.

---

1. "G. K. Chesterton Quotes," *goodreads*, www.goodreads.com/author/quotes/7014283.G_K_Chesterton.
2. "Taking a Fence Down," *The Society of G. K. Chesterton*, www.chesterton.org/taking-a-fence-down/.
3. "The Everlasting Man," *Wikipedia*, en.wikipedia.org/wiki/The_Everlasting_Man

The Christian ideal has not been tried and found wanting. It has been found difficult; and left untried.

The true soldier fights not because he hates what is in front of him, but because he loves what is behind him.

The way to love anything is to realize that it may be lost.

Poets have been mysteriously silent on the subject of cheese.[4]

Having said all this, to me the most far-reaching example of Chesterton's way with words was how he took the proverb we translated in Spanish class about the horse and its teeth, the one about gifts and windfall, and scaled it upward by many magnitudes. "You should not," Chesterton memorably said, "look a gift universe in the mouth."[5] What's true of a gift horse, he's saying, must be true of *everything*. Our lives, our existence, the universe—for all the flaws, the pain, the trouble—are a windfall.

Are we capable of seeing and comprehending this? Can we cosmically scale this notion about the proverbial gift horse up to the universal heights Chesterton suggests? Even amid what might be a challenging day, consider it. Approach the day with fierce Chestertonian pleasure, intoxicated with things just as they are, not as you wish they were, and recognizing that, in essence, it's all a gift. Love today with the knowledge that what is loved may be someday lost, and always be mindful of the remarkable inkiness of ink, the wetness of water, the steeliness of steel, and the unutterable muddiness of mud.

Gracias a Dios por todas tus bendiciones. Amen.

---

4. All quotes from "G. K. Chesterton Quotes," *goodreads*.
5. "G. K. Chesterton," famousquotefrom.com/g-k-chesterton/.

The Holy Act of Noticing

Earth's crammed with heaven,
And every common bush afire with God;
But only he who sees, takes off his shoes,
The rest sit round it and pluck blackberries . . .
—Elizabeth Barrett Browning,
Aurora Leigh, Book 7

One of the many things I'd do if I were able to rerun my college experience would be to spend more time inside the Armstrong Browning Library on the campus of Baylor University. My dad first pointed out the building to me when I was eight as we watched a parade of colorful and amusing floats roll down Speight Avenue before the Bears' homecoming game. I was intrigued by the library's regal look and wondered who this Armstrong and Browning might be. Not too long after that, as a student there, I passed the impressive structure regularly on the way to classes, but somehow I only found my way inside once or twice.

The beautiful building was the lifelong dream of Dr. A. J. Armstrong, who chaired Baylor's English Department from 1912 to 1952.[1] Construction began in 1948, and now the library houses the largest collection of original letters, manuscripts, and books related to the Victorian poets Robert and Elizabeth Barrett Browning in the

---

1. "History: Armstrong Browning Library & Museum," *Baylor University*, library.web.baylor.edu/visit/armstrong-browning-library-museum/about/history.

world, much of it procured by Armstrong and his wife Mary, with the help of the Brownings' only son, Pen, during the early part of the twentieth century.

If I ask myself now why I didn't take advantage of all the library had to offer back then, the practical answer is that I wasn't an English major, so it sort of felt off-limits. The granite steps, the vibrant stained glass, the rich walnut interiors, the intricacies in the ceiling, the brass inlays within the terrazzo floors, the particularly academic brand of silence that swelled inside—it seemed well above my station as a young undergrad. Maybe it was, but I shouldn't have missed it so entirely, as the Brownings are perhaps the most accomplished literary couple of all time. And there—at the corner of 8th and Speight—one can examine the penmanship of their romantic correspondence, analyze original manuscripts of their poetry, hold a number of first editions of their books, and look through untold volumes of material from their personal libraries.

And though it's Robert Browning's bones that are interred under the slate in Poet's Corner at Westminster Abbey, most experts agree that Elizabeth's lifetime of work far surpasses his. She is perhaps best remembered for the line, "How do I love thee, let me count the ways," which she wrote to him during their courtship.[2] But just a few years after unleashing her stirring sonnets into the world, she published a novel-length epic poem called *Aurora Leigh*, "into which," she said, "my highest convictions upon Life and Art have entered." It is in *Aurora Leigh* that Elizabeth Barrett Browning wrote these lines:

> Earth's crammed with heaven,
> And every common bush afire with God;
> But only he who sees, takes off his shoes,
> The rest sit round it and pluck blackberries . . .[3]

---

2. Elizabeth Barrett Browning, *Sonnets from the Portuguese and Other Love Poems* (New York: Doubleday, 1990), number 43.

3. Elizabeth Barrett Browning, *Aurora Leigh*, annotated ed. (Oxford University Press: 2008).

What other Victorian poet would select the unpretentious, even indelicate, yet muscular word "crammed" to express such a sacred thought, then juxtapose it with a biblical example, a Mosaic reference concerning what could be called the holy act of "noticing"? Ancient rabbinical commentaries on Exodus written in Hebrew (which was a language Elizabeth learned to read as a teenager along with Latin, Greek, and Italian) point out that the burning thing Moses came upon in the wilderness was not a large tree but a simple thorn bush.[4] That is to say, this was not a high-production-value miracle or a sublime divine appearance. It was a shrub on fire, with no real need for Moses to pay it any mind. Some rabbis suggest it may have even taken him days to realize the bush was not being consumed before he turned aside from his everyday shepherding duties to notice the "common bush afire with God."[5] But when he did, it changed everything. Soon he was barefoot in the sacred presence of Yahweh.

We miss a lot. We daily walk by remarkable things like the one at the corner of 8th Street and Speight Avenue in Waco. There are places we fail to enter and everyday wonders with which we fail to engage. We miss that the earth is crammed with heaven. If we would just notice it, we might come to recognize that we are always on holy ground. Maybe it would help if, every once in a while, we took off our shoes, looked around, and let ourselves become astonished.

God, today, let me not miss it. Amen.

---

4. "The Burning Bush," *HERZL-NER TAMID*, January 18, 2020, h-nt.org/2020/01/19/the-burning-bush/.
5. Ibid.

37

Astonishing

Oh my goodness!
—*Churchill Downs track announcer Larry Collmus*

Every so often, a sequence of events occurs that leaves me face to face with a failure of which I'm sadly guilty. I'm not sure what to call it, but it's marked by an inadequate appreciation of the myriad wonders passing me by each day. It's a mindset—a posture of the spirit perhaps—that tends to mis-categorize the miraculous as prosaic, the extraordinary as commonplace. I resist being astonished.

The 2022 Kentucky Derby took place in Louisville between 6:57 pm EST and 7:00 pm EST on May 7. Chuck Culpepper and Glynn Hill of the *Washington Post* described what happened within that brief span:

> The stuff of irrational daydreams and sugarplum fairies and future books and future movies and deathless wonder happened Saturday evening at the 148th Kentucky Derby, where a colossal stretch duel yielded suddenly and shockingly to an alternative reality. There, as favorites Epicenter and Zandon battled one another . . . in the fumes of the stretch, an interloper appeared along the rail. Rich Strike, who did not even get into the Kentucky Derby until Friday morning . . . and who went off at 80-1, materialized and capitalized on the others' dogged wane.[1]

---

1. Chuck Culpepper and Glynn A. Hill, "Rich Strike, an 80-1 shot, wins the Kentucky Derby in a stunner," *Washington Post*, May 7, 2022, www.washingtonpost.com/sports/2022/05/07/kentucky-derby/.

If you've not seen this race with track announcer Larry Collmus's voice in your ears (as I now have some twenty times), you must.² It's incredible—a chestnut thoroughbred, the longest of longshots, weaving from the back of the field as if in a videogame, then accelerating into an outlandish gear over the last furlong of the track through a thick density of equine traffic to cross the finish line first.

"Rich Strike is coming up on the inside!" Collmus exclaims in the final seconds of the race. *"Oh my goodness!"* The horse's owner, an unassuming Oklahoman named Richard Dawson, could barely believe it himself. "I asked my trainer up on the stage, 'Are you sure this is not a dream because it can't be true?'"³ Astonishing.

About twenty-four hours after watching the 2022 Kentucky Derby, I filed into Houston's NRG Stadium with my friend Dan and about 50,000 others—a diverse group of all ages and nationalities—to see a popular British band called Coldplay perform with such genuine elation for two hours that the whole show seemed as if it lasted only fifteen minutes. The last time Coldplay came to Houston was in 2017, the day Hurricane Harvey devastated our city. The show was cancelled. They were supposed to return in 2020, but a pandemic broke out.

Houston Chronicle music critic Joey Guerra described the band's long-awaited return like this: "Sunday night's show inside NRG Stadium was, in a word, joy. Pure joy . . . an explosion of color and sound, of warmth and energy."⁴ And for all the spectacle—the giant multicolored spheres bouncing over the audience, the special effects, the confetti cannons—the most powerful moment of the evening occurred when the band's sweat-drenched singer Chris Martin briefly stopped the show to ask everyone to put down their phones and

---

2. "Kentucky Derby 2022 (Full Race)," *NBC Sports*, available on YouTube, www.youtube.com/watch?v=wIYD42DV3Ro&feature=youtu.be.

3. "Rich Strike owner on winning Kentucky Derby," Facebook video, May 8, 2022, www.facebook.com/kentuckycom/videos/rich-strike-owner-on-winning-kentucky-derby-are-you-sure-this-is-not-a-dream/1095668531159255/?locale=ms_MY.

4. Joey Guerra, "Review: Coldplay finally returns to Houston in a big way at NRG Stadium," May 10, 2022, preview.houstonchronicle.com/music/coldplay-finally-returns-to-houston-in-a-big-way-17159007.

simply be present, reveling in an unfolding moment. "Life is short," he said. "Let's be in it together." As he launched into a song called "A Sky Full of Stars,"[5] what ensued felt like a small miracle—a stadium full of people energetically jumping in near synchronous ecstasy with the LED bracelets we'd received coming into the concert lighting up the arena in blue and white as we moved. When Martin threw his hands in the air during the song, on the enormous screens set up over the stage one could easily read the three words tattooed on the inside of his arm: "God Is Love."

Once the gates of astonishment crack open, they often swing wide. Later that night, it struck me that I got home from an astonishing concert by touching a few buttons on an astonishingly efficient application on my astonishingly miraculous phone. An ebullient and kind man named Mustafa in a Nissan Sentra easily located me in the parking lot of a PetSmart store near the stadium and brought me home for a reasonable fee. In the meantime, my wife, who had been 2,000 miles away in Canada all weekend to see family for the first time in three years, flew over a towering mountain range to get back home in just a few hours. Astonishing. It's all astonishing.

Oh, and between the Kentucky Derby and Coldplay, I fell into a stupendous overnight unconsciousness, then miraculously awakened Sunday morning at which time I arose and went to church where, astonishingly, I found myself in the presence of the Creator of fast horses and joyful music, of the sky full of stars, and of Mustafa and me.

God, oh my goodness! Amen.

---

5. Christ Martin, "Sky Full of Stars," *Ghost Stories*, Parlophone Atlantic, 2014. See also "Coldplay: A Sky Full of Stars (Live at River Plate)" www.youtube.com/watch?v=Fpn1imb9qZg (later performance by Coldplay in Buenos Aires).

Heaven and Earth Commingled

To make divine things human and human things divine—such is Bach.

—*Pablo Casals*

Around 1720, though no one is quite sure of the exact date, Johann Sebastian Bach composed a series of suites for the cello. This was unusual at the time as the cello was then considered little more than a background instrument providing a percussive bass line for orchestral performances. No one besides Bach was writing solos for the humble, cumbersome cello at that time.[1] As might have been expected given these circumstances, upon their publication, no one seemed too interested in his unique composition. Many even mistook the almost mathematical progression of notes that flow through the work as a series of mere technical exercises for the plodding instrument.[2] Practically no one played Bach's Cello Suites while he was alive; then the manuscript went missing, and soon they were all but lost to history.[3]

---

1. Eric Siblin, *The Cello Suites: J. S. Bach, Pablo Casals, and the Search for a Baroque Masterpiece* (New York: Grove Atlantic, 2011).
2. Ibid.
3. Steven Isserlis, "Bach to the future . . . how the cello suites survived obscurity to capture the world," *The Guardian*, October 1, 2021, www.theguardian.com/music/2021/oct/01/bach-to-the-future-how-the-cello-suites-survived-

Bach died in 1750, and soon, though it seems inconceivable today, he fell into relative obscurity. It wasn't until 1823 when a German woman named Bella Salomon presented the score of Bach's *St. Matthew Passion* to her fifteen-year-old grandson that the composer's work began to come to light again.[4] The piece so captivated the woman's grandson that he soon dreamt of little else than conducting its performance one day. The dreaming youngster's name was Felix Mendelssohn, and when he realized his aspirations in 1829, staging a performance of *St. Matthew Passion* for an audience in Berlin, it set off a worldwide reexamination of Bach, ushering in a new appreciation for his almost unmatched genius.[5]

However, while Bach himself had been rediscovered, the Cello Suites had gone almost completely missing. Another sixty years passed before a thirteen-year-old boy, a young cello prodigy named Pablo Casals, came upon a single secondhand copy of the Cello Suites in a small Barcelona bookstore.[6] "I began browsing through a bundle of musical scores [and] suddenly came upon a sheaf of pages, crumpled and discolored with age. I looked at them with wonder."[7] The teenager bought the music with money he had earned playing his cello on the Spanish streets, took it home, and began to play it and play it again. And again. It took him twelve years before he felt prepared to perform any of the suites in public, but when he did, everyone went crazy for them and for him as well.[8] "This man does

---

obscurity-to-capture-the-world (excerpt from Isserlis, *The Bach Cello Suites* [London: Faber & Faber, 2021]).

4. Joshua Jacobson, "Book Review: Bach in Berlin Salons," November 19, 2018, www.earlymusicamerica.org/web-articles/book-review-bach-in-berlin-salons/.

5. R. Larry Todd, "Mendelssohn, Felix," in Deane Root, ed., *Grove Music Online*, Oxford University Press. See also Joshua Jacobson, "Book Review: Bach in Berlin Salons," *Early Music America*, November 19, 2018, www.earlymusicamerica.org/web-articles/book-review-bach-in-berlin-salons/.

6. "Yo-Yo Ma—Prelude, Cello Suite No. 1 in G Major," *Song Exploder*, special episode, songexploder.net/transcripts/yo-yo-ma-transcript.pdf. See the official video of Yo-Yo Ma playing this composition on YouTube: www.youtube.com/watch?v=1prweT95Mo0.

7. Isserlis, "Bach to the future."

8. Janet Maslin, "Bewitched by Bach, Bewildered by His Masterpiece," *New York Times*, November 30, 2009, www.nytimes.com/2009/12/01/books/01book.html.

not perform," Norwegian composer Edvard Grieg said of Casals; "he resurrects!"[9] By 1936, Casals had become the most famous cellist in the world and recorded the Cello Suites—the first time anyone had done so. His recording remains beloved today, inspiring cellists like Yo-Yo Ma as well as mere mortals like us. Like me.

I have no real background in music unless my middle school band experience and a handful of piano lessons count (I assure you they do not), and I certainly have no training or expertise in classical music or Bach's compositions. Further, I have no training in neuroscience and am unable to articulate what makes the Cello Suites so enchanting and enduring, but my personal experience listening to them produces this: first, a mysterious consolation of the soul; and second, an equally mysterious alignment between heart and mind that gives me something halfway between a feeling and a thought that is both beautiful and catalyzing, both calming and stirring. Listening to Bach's Cello Suites seems to steer me into a space in which the artistic and the rational somehow blend into a harmonious whole and the barriers separating the terrestrial and the spiritual, the physical and the ephemeral, begin to break down, dissolve, and comingle with one another. I hold no seminary degree either, but it all seems at least tangentially connected to how we experience our faith—in a place somewhere between feeling and thought, the place from which Christ summons us with this prayer to God: "Thy will be done, *on earth as it is in heaven.*"

Indeed, all who pray this prayer on a regular basis are called to inform the physical with the spiritual, to bring a sense of the eternal to the temporal and the sacred to the mundane, to commingle heaven and earth. To bridge this gap, to commingle heaven and earth, is the task and opportunity that God offers to us each day—to make divine things human and human things divine. It is what Bach did, Casals said. So should it be for all of us.

God, today and each day ahead, may your heaven and your earth commingle in me and through me. Amen.

---

9. Ibid.

You're Doing a Good Job

You're doing a good job.
　　—President Harry Truman, addressing a tree on
　　　Maple Street, Independence, Missouri, 1964

President Truman, age eighty, had been out of office for over a decade. Though he remained opinionated, even fiery at times on public matters, by 1964 he was, for the most part, enjoying his Missouri retirement in peace. Writing about this season of Truman's life, his biographer David McCullough related this about the former president:

> Yet on he went, taking his morning walks . . . with Thomas Melton, pastor of First Presbyterian Church . . . the pace a little slower each year, Truman doing most of the talking. Passing an enormous gingko tree on Maple Street, one of the largest, most spectacular trees in town, Truman would customarily speak to it. And what would the president say to the tree, Melton would be asked by a visitor years later. "He'd say, '*You're doing a good job.*'"[1]

Might we all be like this in our twilight—active, pragmatic, grateful, friendly, observant, and present to the world's manifold wonder. Better yet, why wait? Though undeniably much is broken in the world, the things of God—things like the giant gingko tree in Independence, Missouri—are doing a good job with the divine tasks

---

1. David McCullough, *Truman* (New York: Simon & Schuster, 1992).

they've been assigned. Trees cast off both oxygen and pleasant shade. Clouds stir the sky. The moon and stars light the darkness. The oceans roll perpetually onward in time and tide. It must be acknowledged that they're all doing fine work.

But it's not merely the things of earth, sky, and sea that are carrying out God's work. We are as well. We're a resourceful, problem-solving species and—even if it doesn't seem like it sometimes—on balance we're doing a good job too. Allow me to make my case.

My wife Kelly and I took a short trip not long ago. Early in the morning, we boarded a hulking machine made mostly of aluminum yet capable of flight. After reaching a ground speed of nearly 200 mph, engines roaring, the craft was piloted gently and capably into the air, quickly reaching an altitude of 35,000 feet as, under the guidance of air traffic controllers on the ground, we adroitly avoided the other 5,000 jets soaring over the country at the same time. All told, we traveled a good 1,500 miles in three hours before settling down safely, predictably, and routinely amid a waking city of more than eight million people. Everyone involved in the effort performed well, to say the least.

Once there, a genial, hard-working man in a yellow car drove us into the sprawling metropolis. There was traffic, but given the numbers and all the personalities involved, it moved in a remarkably orderly fashion. The roads were well maintained, the signs clear, and I could follow our progress with the global positioning satellite system accessible via a handheld device I happen to own, just as you do. In the distance, the sky-scraping labors of hundreds of architects, thousands of contractors, and tens of thousands of others rose majestically into the heavens. Millions were inside working, living, playing, raising families, solving problems, creating wealth, and serving one another. A lot of people, all things considered, were doing a good job. While New York City has plenty of issues, our problem-solving species was hard at work there performing the various tasks fate had assigned to them. Water ran, electricity was delivered, food was served, parks were manicured, and the subways glided efficiently under the ground. Good work, everyone.

That evening, a cadre of courteous men and women ushered us into a gilded structure located on a bustling street called Broadway where we saw brilliantly skilled actors, who had evidently worked on their craft for years and their lines for months, powerfully and memorably render a timeless story about an ambitious Scottish king who got carried away with his earthly power. Good job, people. Bravo!

Then, upon returning home and to our church's pastoral care work, I soberly listened as families and friends recounted indelible stories about those most dear to them now gone. Two served their country admirably; one served the church with grace. The youngest embodied, unforgettably, a too-brief glimpse of eternal joy. It immensely understates the matter to say they lived well. They lived, each in their own way, ineffably and miraculously.

So may we now highly commend the trees, the earth, the sky, the sea, and also one another with hardy recognition when they—when we—perform well the tasks God has given each of us to accomplish.

"You're doing a good job."

God, help me not forget that so much and so many are performing well. Amen.

If Ruth Could among Alien Corn . . .

> . . . *if Ruth could among alien corn begin the line of Judah that led to David—then what is not possible, and what perfection would be disallowed.*
> —Mark Helprin, "Perfection," in
> The Pacific and Other Short Stories

Mark Helprin is an American novelist who served in the British Merchant Navy, in the Israeli infantry, and then in the Israeli Air Force. He's studied at Harvard, Oxford, and Princeton. He has earned a living as a dishwasher, a factory worker, and a stevedore. He now grows hay on his Virginia farm, but mostly he's a writer. He provides foreign policy commentary for the *Wall Street Journal* and has penned speeches for presidential candidates. Most of the time, he writes arresting short stories and novels that lend credibility to the elusive notion of hope.[1]

Helprin is Jewish. His first novel, *Refiner's Fire*, which tells the tale of Marshall Pearl who was born in 1947 on a sinking ship off the coast of Haifa at the moment the Jewish state was established, revealed Helprin's deep knowledge of both ancient and modern

---

1. Mark Helprin, "The Art of Fiction No. 132," interview by James Linville, *The Paris Review* 126 (Spring 1993), www.theparisreview.org/interviews/1962/the-art-of-fiction-no-132-mark-helprin.

Israel.[2] Poet Joyce Carol Oates, remarking on the sheer beauty of the novel in her 1977 *New York Times* book review, stated that "despite its formidable length, [it] probably should be read aloud." Her praise continued: "it goes on and on, at whim, stringing together feats and jokes and implausibilities, yet is always winning."[3]

The *Times*'s 1983 review of Helprin's next novel, a magical fable titled *Winter's Tale*,[4] noted that

> good and evil lock horns time and again in this work, and evil does not prevail. Men and women of virtue and intellect are regularly awarded honors. Children who die untimely deaths are miraculously raised from the grave. [Even] smoke-cloud disasters . . . are themselves found not lacking in silver linings.[5]

There's a sort of Old Testament quality to Helprin's writing that reminds me of the story of Joseph. The story of Queen Esther. The story of Ruth. The story of the prophet Elisha. The story of Jonah. For in each of these ancient tales, good and evil lock horns time and again and evil does not, in the end, prevail. Joseph is left for dead by his brothers, then wrongly accused of assault and imprisoned, then forgotten. Yet, by the conclusion of the book of Genesis, he has saved two kingdoms and his family. In these centuries-old biblical narratives, men and women of virtue and intellect are awarded honors. Esther, exiled, a pagan king's concubine, becomes queen and then, against all odds, saves her people.

In these revered biblical accounts, children who die untimely deaths are miraculously raised from the grave. Elisha raises a poor woman's little son from the dead. In these historic chapters of the Old

---

2. Mark Helprin, *Refiner's Fire*, 1st ed. (Boston: Mariner Books, 2005).

3. Joyce Carol Oates, "Picaresque Tale," *New York Times*, January 1, 1978, www.nytimes.com/1978/01/01/archives/picaresque-tale-refiners-fire.html.

4. Mark Helprin, *Winter's Tale*, 1st ed. (Boston: Mariner Books, 2005).

5. Benjamin de Mott, "*Winter's Tale*," book review, *New York Times*, September 4, 1983, www.nytimes.com/1983/09/04/books/winters-tale.html. See also "A Piercing Sense of the Beautiful: On Mark Helprin's *Winter's Tale*," Book Mark, December 28, 2017, bookmarks.reviews/a-piercing-sense-of-the-beautiful-on-mark-helprins-winters-tale/.

Testament, silver linings and crucial lessons are detectable in many of the disaster tales, such as Noah's ark and Jonah and the whale. Time after time, there are miraculous escapes from catastrophe and incredible returns from exile. Redemption cascades from suffering. Families regather. Nations rise again.

The story of Ruth begins in bitter sorrow; she is bereft, a refugee in a foreign land. But she demonstrates considerable pluck, asserting a remarkable agency over awful events amid a new community. With a beautiful marriage and the birth of a child, her story ends with these words: "And they named him Obed. He was the father of Jesse, the father of David." In these venerated stories, God strings together—through the lives of these heroes and heroines of the faith—improbable feats, jokes (most often at the expense of the arrogant and powerful), and implausibilities that somehow, even after thousands and thousands of years, still ring true to us.

Our lives sometimes don't feel heroic but mundane, pocked by detours and unfortunate off-ramps. But what if we really came to believe in the comeback stories of Joseph, Esther, Elisha, Jonah, Ruth, or even Peter Lake or Marshall Pearl? What if we—thoughtfully, passionately, with large and expansive souls, and under God's guidance and our own agency—committed anew, against the odds, to becoming true heroes and heroines of our faith?

It seems that the best stories of the past and the best stories of today brazenly sound the heroic theme that suffering can be redeemed, God can do much with little, the odds can be overcome, and we are a part of God's continuing miraculous epic when we believe that "if Ruth could among alien corn begin the line of Judah that led to David—then what is not possible, and what perfection would be disallowed."[6]

God, help me to believe in heroic possibilities. Amen.

---

6. Mark Helprin, "Perfection," *The Pacific and Other Short Stories* (Penguin Press, 2004). See also Helprin, "Perfection: A Story," *Commentary*, October 2004, www.commentary.org/articles/mark-helprin-2/perfection-a-story/.

Friday

Imagination

And God said, "Let the water teem with living creatures, and let birds fly through above the earth across the vault of the sky...." And there was evening, and there was morning—the fifth day. (Genesis 1:20, 23)

Saints and Poets

The saints and poets maybe—they do some.
—Stage Manager in *Thornton Wilder's* Our Town

What if you had died yesterday but were then today somehow granted life again? Think about it. What if you had passed away last night, but this morning you were restored to the circumstances you are in right this minute? With the family you have. With the friends you have. In the community where you live. With your health even such as it may be. What if you were restored to the present with respect to all these things? Repatriated to this place. Brought back to this particular moment. How much would you savor this altogether ordinary "right now"?

As I write this, one of New York's Broadway theaters is preparing to stage a revival of Thornton Wilder's *Our Town*, which won the Pulitzer Prize for Drama in 1938.[1] Jim Parsons will portray a character known in the play simply as the Stage Manager, a sort of narrator who sometimes interacts with the other characters. The show is set in 1903 in a sleepy little town called Grover's Corner. It starts with the Stage Manager introducing us to a few of the town's citizens, including a girl named Emily Webb and a boy named George Gibbs. The audience sees Emily's mother fixing breakfast before Emily and her brother go off to school. Men and women are working around

---

1. Thornton Wilder, *Our Town* (New York: Harper Perennial Modern Classics, 2003).

town or at home. It's as ordinary as a day could be. That's the whole first act.

In the second act, perhaps even less happens. Emily and George, now a few years older, get married, buy a farm, and struggle along with the rest of the town with the mundane matters of life. So little happens in the second act that an audience member might be forgiven for asking, "So how did this show win a Pulitzer Prize?"

Well, there's a third act.

In the remarkable last section of the play, set a few years later, we learn that Emily has died during childbirth. She observes her own funeral taking place in the town cemetery and even speaks to some of the other dearly departed citizens of Grover's Corner, including Mrs. Gibbs, George's mother, who has also passed away. There in the graveyard, Emily sees George suffering and laments to Mrs. Gibbs, "It won't be the same to George without me, but it's a lovely farm." Then Emily asks Mrs. Gibbs, "Live people don't understand, do they?" Mrs. Gibbs replies, "No, dear—not very much."

Emily is then told if she chooses to do so, she can return to a single day in her life. Mrs. Gibbs advises Emily not to choose the most momentous of her days but rather the least important one. "It will be important enough," she tells Emily. Emily decides on her twelfth birthday, and as the day unfolds, she is so overcome by what she experiences that she finally turns to the Stage Manager, who is standing off to the side, and with mounting urgency complains to him, "It goes too fast. We don't have time to look at one another." She then breaks down sobbing. "I didn't realize," she says, "all that was going on and we never noticed." At the end of the third act, through her tears, Emily asks him, "Do any human beings ever realize life while they live it?" The Stage Manager replies, "No." But then he thinks a moment and adds, "The saints and poets maybe—they do some."

I admit that the question, "What if I had died yesterday?" can be a pretty grim one to ask ourselves each morning, so maybe we can begin to think more like saints, more like poets, by asking another sort of question. Try this one: How can I make the situation I'm in today—the one I'm in right now—*holy*?

It might mean looking around to notice a fallen leaf, the slope of an anthill, or the construction of a wasp's nest. It might mean slowing down to really look into the eyes of the person in front of you. It might mean including someone standing off to the side who has been left out. Maybe it's reconnecting with the family you have or a friend you've forgotten. It might mean savoring your breakfast a little more, listening to someone's story more intently, sending a note to someone who has lost a loved one recently, resting in silence, or just letting yourself laugh more deeply at something funny. Or it might just mean ruminating on the question for a bit to realize what is going on that you never noticed before and, simply by noticing it, make it holy.

God, help me imaginatively sanctify this very moment. Amen.

Jude and Revelation

Na . . . na . . . na . . . na-na-na-na . . . na-na-na-na . . .
—*"Hey Jude," Paul McCartney*

It was midnight on a Friday when a local radio station began rolling out the Top 100 songs of all time. I was about ten and staying overnight at a friend's house with five others. We all played on the same youth basketball team, and despite the fact that we had a game the next morning at eight, while the others began to doze off, I found myself mesmerized more and more each hour by what emerged from the radio. Finally, just before dawn, with my friends still asleep, the DJ introduced the top song.

> Hey Jude,
> Don't make it bad,
> Take a sad song and make it better.
> Remember to let her into your heart,
> Then you can start to make it better.[1]

Then, along with the simple piano chords, a gently jangling tambourine joined in, hitting the downbeats with the quiet strumming ring of an acoustic guitar in the background. Soon perfectly harmonized voices—John Lennon's, George Harrison's—were added.

---

1. The Beatles, "Hey Jude," New York, Apple, 1968.

> Hey Jude, Don't be afraid.
> You were made to go out and get her.
> The minute you let her under your skin
> Then you begin to make it better

The music stirred further, building, holding back, rising, and turning again until, at about the three-minute mark, still less than halfway through the song, there was an incredible sonic lift:

> Na . . . na . . . na . . . na-na-na-na
> Na-na-na-na . . . Hey Jude

When I was a little kid, my favorite Beatles songs were the deceptively simple Ringo tunes like "Yellow Submarine" and "Octopus's Garden," along with early Lennon and McCartney hits like the ebullient "Eight Days a Week" and "Love Me Do." I'd heard "Hey Jude" without really listening to it. But now it stirred that singing feeling of life inside me. At the end of a long night of listening to music, it felt more discovered than composed—a revelation.

"Everyone knows it. Consider that," James Campion writes in his terrific book, *Take a Sad Song: The Emotional Currency of Hey Jude*.[2] "Everyone. All over the planet . . . . For over half a century it has been a communal celebration of song with no language barrier. Infectious. Commanding. Unforgettable . . . ."

"Hey Jude" was released in August 1968 and remained at the top of the US Billboard charts for an astonishing nine weeks. It hit #1 in eighteen other countries as well. Its duration—seven minutes and eleven seconds—was unprecedented for a pop song.[3] Paul McCartney, the song's composer, acknowledged, "It wasn't intended to go on that long."[4] But he, along with John, George, and Ringo, evidently knew what they had. They had ears, after all. A lament, a desire, an intimate yet universal pep talk during an otherwise dark

---

2. James Campion, *Take a Sad Song: The Emotional Currency of "Hey Jude"* (London: Backbeat Books, 2022).
3. Ibid.
4. Ibid.

year—even now, more than half a century later, the song produces abject joy in some and brings others to tears, and sometimes both at the same time. When played live—whenever, wherever—it prompts powerful, memorable, beautiful singalongs. It's one of those tunes that, because you've heard it all your life, you forget how incredibly life-affirming it is.

> And anytime you feel the pain, hey Jude, refrain,
> Don't carry the world upon your shoulders.

Though not a religious person, McCartney grew up singing in the boys' choir and playing the bells at St. Barnabas Anglican Church in Liverpool and, because it appears in the English Book of Common Prayer, would certainly have sung a 1907 liturgical piece written by English composer John Ireland called *Te Deum Laudamus in F Major*.[5] If you listen to the beginning of Ireland's *Te Deum*, it's clear McCartney, perhaps unconsciously, drew from these first few notes when he wrote "Hey Jude."[6] Likewise, while the words of McCartney's song famously reflect a conversation between Paul and John Lennon's young son, Julian—the Jude referenced in the lyrics[7]—it's interesting to note that St. Jude is the patron saint of lost causes. Surely this wasn't lost on the song's singularly brilliant composer.

What isn't in doubt, though, is that McCartney's lyrics and vocal performance take the listener on a pilgrimage through what at first seems to be sad song but ends with an epic and sublime coda—what those in the church might call an amen cadence and what Campion in his book calls the "infinity part" (the na-na-na's), joyfully reinforcing the song's message of perseverance in life and in love, assuring not only a young boy but all the rest of us that we're going to get through this.

---

5. Ibid.
6. Hear the Choir & Choristers of Grace Church in Providence perform the song: www.youtube.com/watch?v=EY-AI1tXGmw.
7. Campion, *Take a Sad Song*, 62–63.

For well you know that it's a fool who plays it cool
By making his world a little colder.

God, thank you today for the incredible imagination of our artists, the wonder and revelation of music, and that singing feeling of life. Amen.

Looking for the Scintilla

scin-til-la (noun): a tiny trace or spark of a specified quality or feeling.

Scintilla. Simply the way the word sounds conveys a measure of its meaning. It's wispy, ephemeral, glancing. A scintilla of evidence. A scintilla of doubt. Perhaps it's not even present. You have to look closely. Maybe even squint a little. You have to attend the circumstances to detect that tiny trace, that spark. Even then it might not be there. Look again. Maybe it is.

The first time I heard this word was in law school. The professors who lectured to us, the judicial opinions we read, and the whole epistemological philosophy we were asked to undertake encouraged us to embrace this word, to ask questions: *Is there a scintilla of factual evidence in the record to support the proposition at hand? Is it there? Or is it not?*

The approach reinforced an idea I'd heard before—that one doesn't have to become a lawyer to benefit from such a legal education because it immerses one not in *what* to think but in an overall *way* of thinking that rewards close examination. This method helps one spot issues that might ordinarily be missed and then articulate the possibilities around them. The project is designed to hone one's aptitude to detect with rigor and precision and then attend those "hard-to-spot-unless-you're-looking-for-them" things that might prompt even more questions, more investigation, more inquiry—all in service to discovering the truth about the matter at hand.

The Israeli Defense Force has a practice called The Tenth Man.[1] It's been explained to me like this: When strategizing and planning, if everyone in the room agrees on a certain path or policy, the playbook of the organization dictates that someone present must step up and argue the other side, *against* the policy, advocating with all the intellectual firepower they can bring to bear on the matter. This requirement, even if it doesn't change the proposed course of action, effectively surfaces issues that might not otherwise be considered, bringing attention to obscure or hidden possibilities that might be overlooked. The practice allows a fuller vetting of the policy, ensuring that the decision is not merely the product of momentum, peer pressure, or groupthink. Just as a law school education is to an individual, the Tenth Man practice is to an organization. It's about broadening, expanding, and focusing one's vision on what's really there so that the scintilla, the trace, the glimmer of something more, something else, won't be missed.

Do you have something like this for your faith? An approach? A practice that attunes you to what is really there so that you don't miss something? I've given some thought to something that is perhaps a fanciful theory, but it touches closely on this idea of *scintilla*.

Here's the theory: What if, just maybe, God is speaking, revealing the Divine to us in all sorts of ways all the time, but we're not quite hearing or seeing them? That is, we can't quite make out these always-present, ongoing revelations because we're not looking and listening closely and critically enough. What if we're set up, in a sense, on the wrong frequency? What if the prescription we're using for our vision, for our 'divine-detector,' has gotten a click or two off? My theory goes on to imagine that one day we'll see our lives like one of those movies where, near the end of the film in a sort of montage, a number of previous scenes are rolled back and shown again from a subtly different perspective, and we will then pick up on scintillas,

---

1. See "How Israeli intelligence failures led to a 'devil's advocate' role," excerpt from William Kaplan's *Why Dissent Matters: Because Some People See Things the Rest of Us Miss* (McGill-Queen's University Press, 2017). Available at *Toronto Star*, www.thestar.com/news/insight/2017/05/21/how-israeli-intelligence-failures-led-to-a-devils-advocate-role.html.

traces, artifacts of God as having been right there all along—clearly detectable had we attended our circumstances a little more closely. In retrospect, we won't believe we missed all of them.

Maybe approaching each day sensitive to the winsome if not whimsical idea that God is broadcasting to us in a lively way all the time might spark our imagination, our minds, and our hearts—catalyzing, reanimating, reigniting, and replenishing—in just the way we need right now.

Look for a scintilla of God right before you today. Then attend it. Fully vet the possibility. Let it prompt more questions, more investigation, more inquiry. It might lead to the discovery of more truth about the matter at hand.

God, today I ask for that imaginative spark—the capability, the vision, the radar—to detect a scintilla of the divine right before me. Amen.

More

There is no limit to beauty, no saturation point in design, no end to the material.

—Salvatore Ferragamo

Cary Grant once said, "It's better to buy one good pair of shoes than four cheap ones. One pair made of fine leather," he continued, "can outlast four inferior pairs, and if well cared for, will proclaim your good judgment and taste no matter how old they become."[1] Based on this sound advice, a few years ago I purchased on sale from a local department store a pair of size 8 black dress shoes made by Salvatore Ferragamo. I've had them re-soled a couple of times. The leather remains as supple as ever, and they still wear well.

Born in 1898 to an impoverished family in a small town in southern Italy—a town whose name, Bonita, translates roughly in English as *beautiful*—Salvatore Ferragamo, the eleventh of fourteen children, became fascinated at an early age with how shoes are made.[2] As a toddler, he used to venture down the street from his home to the workshop of a local craftsman to watch him cobble

---

1. Julia Guerra, "Who Is Salvatore Ferragamo? Everything You Need to Know about the Famous Fashion Designer," *InStyle*, August 29, 2022, www.instyle.com/fashion/who-is-salvatore-ferragamo. See also "The Story of Salvatore Ferragamo," *Uncommon & Curated*, uncommonandcurated.com/2022/11/04/the-story-of-salvatore-ferragamo/; and Luca Guadagnino, *Salvatore: Shoemaker of Dreams*, Sony Pictures, 2020.

2. Ibid.

shoes together.³ Then at age nine, as two of his sisters neared their first communion, young Salvatore stayed up all night to make shoes for both of them to wear. Recognizing his son's passion and how the girls' handmade shoes pleased Salvatore's mother, his father allowed him to move to Naples at age twelve to study the trade. After a few years there, Salvatore returned home to open a shoe store in his parents' basement, earning a modest living.⁴

At age seventeen, Salvatore immigrated to the United States, and following a brief stint working at a boot factory in Boston, he moved to California where he opened a small shop in Hollywood serving the burgeoning silent movie industry. He created sandals for Cecil B. DeMille's 1923 silent film *The Ten Commandments*, made cowboy boots for early westerns, and was soon personally designing footwear for starlets such as Jean Harlow, Mary Pickford, and Greta Garbo.⁵

Refusing to accept that shoes could not be both beautiful and comfortable at the same time, Ferragamo studied anatomy at the University of Southern California before returning to Italy in 1927 where he continued to experiment with his innovative designs.⁶ Using sunny yellows, intense reds, emerald greens, and deep blues, he began combining such lively colors in ways that had many calling his remarkable creations nothing less than wearable works of art.

In Florence, Ferragamo soon applied for a series of patents related to his designs, began hiring local artisans to meet the growing customer demand for his shoes, and eventually found himself at the helm of a successful global-scale enterprise. All the while, he continued to cement his reputation as shoemaker to the stars, creating ballet flats for Audrey Hepburn, crafting strappy stilettos for Marilyn Monroe, and employing a variety of other designs for famous customers like Ingrid Bergman, Katharine Hepburn, and Rita Hayworth.⁷

All his life, Salvatore Ferragamo insisted on the highest quality of leather, fabrics, and thread that he used along with an unmatched

---

3. Ibid.
4. Ibid.
5. Ibid.
6. Ibid.
7. Ibid.

standard of craftsmanship to push the imaginative boundaries of his chosen art form. "There is no limit to beauty," he said, "no saturation point in design, no end to the material."[8]

While Ferragamo's creations related mainly to what we might place on our feet, God's creative field encompasses not only the foot itself but also so much more—our entire bodies. Consider how the parts of your body work in concert with one another. Consider all the places your feet have taken you. Even a brief consideration of all this might prompt us to echo Ferragamo's words but direct them in praise of God's own handiwork: "There is no limit to beauty, no saturation point in design, no end to the material."

On an even more expansive level, whether we are looking up into interstellar space through a powerful telescope, into the tiniest measure of matter with an electron microscope, across the boundaries and curious nature of time, or into the inexplicable mystery of consciousness, there's always more. More to astound. More to astonish. More of God's creative genius and infinite ability to produce wonders without end. More. More. And more. All born of an unimaginable love, an unfathomable generative power, and an all-encompassing and everlasting grace. Look down. Look down in awe at your feet, whether barefoot, ill-fitted, or merrily shod, and consider this a bit more. You stand on sacred ground.

God, no limit. No saturation point. No end. Oh, my soul. Amen and amen.

---

8. *AZ Quotes,* /www.azquotes.com/quote/641861.

Observe

I don't think many people fully understand the value of observing.
—Sir Alexander Ferguson

The season I enjoyed coaching little league the most was when my son Charlie was ten. I call it the year of the Iron Pigs. I'd drafted a terrific team of kids, and we had cool navy blue caps emblazoned with a fierce pig, silver rivets bolted formidably to its neck. I'd also assembled a great coaching staff to help me—dads as ridiculously serious about the endeavor as I was; not only were they fantastic people but they also knew baseball better than I did. As the season began, they handled the drills in practice, developing the boys' skills with patience and good humor and allowing me to oversee the whole operation from a higher level. With their help, I had the luxury of thinking ahead, considering the big picture of what we wanted to accomplish over the season, all the while ready to jump in with time and real presence when and where I was needed most. The Iron Pigs grew into a superb team, deeply invested in one another. Even though the season ended with a heart-breaking, extra-inning loss in the championship game that, honest, I never replay in my mind at all anymore, we had a memorable year together.

When Alex Ferguson took over as manager of the Manchester United football club in 1986, the team hadn't won a title in two decades. They were about to be relegated to a lower division, which is what happens in the English Premier League when a team tanks or underperforms over time. However, instead of relegation, owing largely to Ferguson's splendid leadership—over the next twenty-seven years—Manchester United won thirty-eight domestic and international titles to become one of the most storied franchises in all of sports. What John Wooden is to basketball, Connie Mack is to baseball, and Vince Lombardi is to American football, Alex Ferguson is to soccer. This success led Harvard Business School's Anita Elberse to fly across the Atlantic to study his management style and write an article about it for the *Harvard Business Journal*.[1]

Perhaps what's most striking in her compelling article is a story about a Manchester United assistant coach who persuaded Ferguson to trust him with more responsibility. Though originally wary of ceding his authority to an assistant, Ferguson later said, "It was the best thing I ever did," as it freed him to perform his job at a higher and deeper level.[2] He could now simply observe his team and respond where his expertise was most needed. "What you can pick up by watching is incredibly valuable. Once I stepped out of the bubble, I became more aware of a range of details . . . a change in a player's habits or a sudden dip in his enthusiasm."[3] With these observations, he could go deeper with his players and staff. Was there a family problem? Was a player struggling financially? Was he tired? Injured? Was it something else? "I don't think," Ferguson concluded, "many people fully understand the value of observing."[4]

Do you have this luxury? The time and the space to step back and observe what might be going on in the lives of those around you and then respond to it? Or perhaps even to observe what's going on at a deeper level within the little operation you call your own life? Yeah, me neither, but we should.

We don't have to read too far into the gospel before Jesus starts referring to something he calls the kingdom of God. You'll notice that when he brings it up, he doesn't seem to be talking about some

---

1. Anita Elberse, "Ferguson's Formula," *Harvard Business Review*, October 2013, hbr.org/2013/10/fergusons-formula.
2. Ibid.
3. Ibid.
4. Ibid.

heavenly locale but rather an unseen realm that—though it's right before us, among us, even within us—we only truly experience when we remove ourselves from the bubble we think of as our regular lives and *observe* life in a new and different way. He seems to be saying that there's both a higher level and a deeper level of life placed on offer to us, embedded into the reality in which we exist, if we could only detect and access it. And Ferguson's suggestion about the value of *just observing* strikes me as crucial to this endeavor to which Christ points us.

This week, consider reserving some imaginative space and the energy, then—with intention—giving yourself the time to detect this hidden kingdom of God, which Christ tells us is right in front of us, among us, even inside us. And when you sense it near, just observe, and see what happens next.

God, help me step outside my bubble to more deeply, more imaginatively observe your kingdom at hand. Amen.

Please Remain Seated

If I just sit there long enough, something will happen.
—*Anne Lamott*

Once it was for surreptitiously shuffling a serving of stewed squash off my dinner plate through the window of our kitchen and into an adjacent flower bed. More than once it was for quarrelling with my sisters about the phone—there was only a single line for the whole family back then. Quite a few times it was for fighting with my brother. But each instance of misbehavior would lead to a stiff parental reprimand—one that typically involved being sent to my room. Once there, I was told to sit still. To stay put and think. And while it's been a long time since that happened, sometimes, for all sorts of reasons, not just punitive ones, we need to be instructed to do that.

Just sit still.

Anne Lamott is a novelist and the author of several nonfiction books driven by deeply spiritual themes about grace, mercy, redemption, and hope. She was awarded a Guggenheim Fellowship in the mid-eighties when she was thirty years old and, for the last forty years, has continued to write with an unflinching devotion to honesty and the truth with a uniquely quirky wit. She writes about "human hearts, spiritual transformation, families, secrets, wonder, craziness," always aiming to, as she puts it, "throw the lights on a little." You get a real sense of her faith and what's most important to her simply by reviewing the titles of her books. Here are just a few: *Traveling*

Mercies: Some Thoughts on Faith; *Plan B: Further Thoughts on Faith*; *Grace (Eventually)*; *Help, Thanks, Wow: The Three Essential Prayers*; *Hallelujah Anyway: Rediscovering Mercy*; and *Dusk, Night, Dawn: On Revival and Courage*.[1]

Back in 1993, Lamott published her first memoir-like effort called *Operating Instructions: A Journal of My Son's First Year* in which she told a story from her own childhood about her older brother. Ten years old at the time, he was struggling with a school report on birds that had been assigned three months before but was now due the next day.

> . . . he was at the kitchen table close to tears, surrounded by binder paper and pencils and unopened books about birds, immobilized by the hugeness of the task ahead. Then my father sat down beside him put his arm around my brother's shoulder, and said, *"Bird by bird, buddy. Just take it bird by bird."*[2]

The story so captured her readers' attention and imagination that Lamott called her next book *Bird by Bird: Some Instructions on Writing and Life*.[3] In it, she recounts how we so easily become overwhelmed by big tasks. Whether it's in writing a book or taking on any other ambitious endeavor, breaking things down into smaller "bird by bird" increments, she sagely advised, helps us to get started. As far as finishing such a project, Lamott, while writing that she wished she could offer a foolproof code-cracking secret to accomplishing one's goals, acknowledges that there's really no mystery to it. You simply have to sit down and, as she puts it, "keep your butt in the chair."[4]

---

1. Steve Lowery, "Anne Lamott's wit and wisdom on display at Carpenter Center," *The Hi-Lo*, March 9, 2020, lbpost.com/hi-lo/anne-lamotts-wit-and-wisdom-on-display-at-carpenter-center-saturday.

2. Anne Lamott, *Operating Instructions: A Journal of My Son's First Year* (repr., Anchor, 2005).

3. Anne Lamott, *Bird by Bird: Some Instructions on Writing and Life* (Knopf Doubleday Publishing, 1995).

4. Kurt Anderson, "Anne Lamott: Beyond Bird by Bird," *The World: Studio 360*, March 16, 2012, theworld.org/stories/2012-03-16/anne-lamott-beyond-bird-bird.

Chuck Close, a painter, photographer, and visual artist at the forefront of the photorealism art movement during the sixties and seventies, expressed a similar notion. "Inspiration is for amateurs," he said. "The rest of us just show up and get to work."[5] Close, a recipient of the 2000 National Medal of the Arts, was suggesting that the idea of that sudden lightning strike of pure genius, or a creative muse suddenly arriving at one's doorstep to bestow a brilliant idea, is mythical. It doesn't work that way. "All the best ideas," he said, "come out of the process. They come out of the work itself."[6]

Sometimes, just sitting there, thinking, working, grinding it out seems a lot like eating our vegetables, our stewed squash, but as Anne Lamott—with her remarkable faith and over a dozen terrific books to her credit—once told an audience, "If I just sit there long enough, something will happen."[7]

> *God, help me remain in my seat and just sit still—something, remarkably and remarkable, will happen. Amen.*

---

5. Maria Popova, "Chuck Close on Creativity, Work Ethic, and Problem-Solving vs. Problem-Creating," *The Marginalian*, December 12, 2012, www.themarginalian.org/2012/12/27/chuck-close-on-creativity/.

6. "Inspiration Is for Amateurs," *Design Sojourn*, November 1, 2010, designsojourn.com/inspiration-is-for-amateurs/.

7. "Book Summary: Bird by Bird," *Paminy*, paminy.com/book-summary-bird-instructions-writing-life/. See also "1994 Anne Lamott 'Bird by Bird' at the San Francisco Public Library," *YouTube*, March 1, 1994, youtu.be/U-llneDcXPo.

Banking on Hope

George Banks and all he stands for will be saved. Maybe not in life, but in imagination. Because that's what we storytellers do. We restore order with imagination. We instill hope again and again and again.
—*from the film* Saving Mr. Banks

I saw Walt Disney's *Mary Poppins* as a little kid in an enormous movie house—the Windsor Theatre in Houston's Galleria area—before the Galleria was even a thing. I recall Dick Van Dyke dancing with animated penguins and the happy ending with the kites in the sky before Mary floats away with her umbrella. I also remember a few years later, not too far from the old Windsor after they'd built the Galleria, standing in a line wrapped around the shopping center's indoor ice-skating rink to see a new movie that had just come out called *Jaws*. Based on the not-too-subtle movie poster and the buzz, I knew it concerned a giant man-eating shark, and yet, in the end, it too had a happy ending (at least for most of the characters). Not long after that, I was queuing up again around the same ice-skating rink to see another movie with a happy ending. One called *Star Wars*.

I love the movies, enjoy a variety of cinematic genres, and welcome all sorts of storylines, but I admit I'm partial to the happy ending. I don't need every loose end tied up with implausible perfection, but when I sit through a film that ends sadly, cynically, or without any sense of redemption, I usually find myself disappointed. I leave asking why, with all the real sadness, trouble, and defeat in the world,

I spent the last two hours of my life in the theatre absorbing more of it.

Saving Mr. Banks is a movie released in 2013 that tells the story of author Pamela "P.L." Travers and Walt Disney's pursuit of the screen rights to her Mary Poppins books.[1] The title of the film refers to George Banks, the father in Travers's Mary Poppins stories whose family the irrepressible Mary comes to serve and eventually save with her enchanting magic, charming personality, and catchy showtunes.

As the movie proceeds—through a series of flashbacks to Miss Travers's childhood in Australia in the early 1900s—we begin to sense that the Mr. Banks character in her books, a banker, is based on her loving, creative, but deeply depressed real-life father, also a banker, whom she adored despite his addictions. We later learn that Travers's real name is Helen Goff and that she's taken her deceased father's first name, Travers, as her pen name. We learn also that when she was seven years old, just before he died, her bright-eyed but no-nonsense aunt had come to live with her family, taking charge of their troubled household. Though she could not save Travers's father, as we follow her aunt's manner, notice her turns of phrases, and spot her umbrella, we're left to conclude that she is the inspiration for Mary Poppins herself.

Near the end of the film, still trying to convince her to trust him, Disney empathetically speaks to Miss Travers about her childhood and her loss, sharing evocative details of his own hardship growing up in Missouri and his complicated relationship with his dad. He urges that she not let the failure to save her own father in real life prevent them from turning a story of personal tragedy into one of redemption.

"In every movie house, all over the world," Disney tells her, "in the eyes and the hearts of my kids, and other kids and their mothers and fathers for generations to come, George Banks will be honored. George Banks will be redeemed. George Banks and all he stands for will be saved. Maybe not in life, but in imagination. Because that's

---

1. *Saving Mr. Banks*, directed by John Lee Hancock, produced by Alison Owen, Ian Collie, Philip Steuer, Walt Disney Pictures, 2013.

what we storytellers do. We restore order with imagination. We instill hope again and again and again."[2]

There's something mystical about the healing power of art. And stories with happy endings, whether in the form of magical fairy tales, epic adventures on the high seas, science-fiction space operas, or even compelling biographical pictures, have a way of making hope seem more credible to us. Of setting things right inside of us. Such stories help us sort out the chaotic real world in which we live. They give us a picture of what we feel deeply in our souls *should* happen, even if it doesn't happen. Embracing the possibility that things can redemptively turn out right both demonstrates our capacity for hope and steels our conviction that, in the end, they will.

God, help me gather the imagination today to truly bank on hope. Amen.

---

2. Ibid.

A New Kind of New

Behold, I make all things new. (Revelation 21:5)

I was about fourteen when I decided I had to have a new bike. I'd always had one of those nubby-tired mountain bikes for roaming around with friends along the dirt trails in the woods near our home, but a terrific movie about bicycle racing called *Breaking Away* had just come out. I was inspired, and what I really wanted now was a road bike.[1] I began to save my lawn-mowing money, and soon made my way to the local Schwinn store to buy a 10-speed. It was a stretch purchase for me and effectively cleaned out all of my savings, but I saw myself riding it far and near for a long time to come.

My first outing was to the Target store a few miles from my house, as I needed a lock and chain to keep my new prized possession safe and sound. I stashed my beautiful new bicycle against a wall behind a big planter in front of the store and hustled inside to make the quick purchase. I was gone only about ten minutes, but when I returned, my bike had disappeared. I looked all around, absorbing that awful, sinking feeling. I had possessed the bicycle for less than twenty-four hours, and now it was gone. My picture of humanity took a hit that day, but, as you might imagine, I couldn't even tell the story about losing the bike without having to answer the question of why I put it at risk in the first place. Fair enough. Lesson learned.

We all like new stuff. Researchers who study the matter have measured the dopamine rush we experience when we receive a gift,

---

1. *Breaking Away*, directed and produced by Peter Yates, 1979.

purchase something we want, or acquire something new. However, just as reliably as those feelings of exhilaration come, immediately the process of wear and tear begins to work on our newly minted prizes. New cars get scratched. New sweaters get stained. New phones are dropped. New jewelry is lost. New homes and the things inside them don't remain perfect for long. And of course, bitterly, sadly, bikes get stolen. Anything new that comes to us in this world is soon and inevitably exposed to the ravages of time, marred by entropy, and made vulnerable to loss and decay. It's just the nature of things. At least, it is in this world.

In the book of Revelation, we're told that God makes all things new, but there's something more here that suggests God is offering us a new kind of new—not the same kind of new that is subject to all manner of decline. In an expanded Greek translation of the passage penned by a scholar named Kenneth Wuest, a slight addition to the verse leads it to read like this: "Behold, I make all things new *in quality*." What this translation might surrender in poetry it returns with some keen insight.[2]

The word "new," when used on its own, fails to express the idea that time will affect the thing in question just like it always does. But the phrase "new in quality" makes us think more deeply. It asks us to consider the qualities of newness without regard to the notion of time. It points us to the elation we feel when we experience something new and good in the instant and holds us there. To say that something is "new in quality" is to say that it durably, eternally maintains its newness—its power to energize and entrance in a way that is unsusceptible to stain, loss, fading, or theft.

The following exercise might help us at least fleetingly experience this idea: the next time you receive a gift you've anticipated or a mail package you've looked forward to, as you open it, pay attention to how you feel. Whatever has come into your hands, consider its newness and what "new in quality" really means and feels like. Linger there as long as you can.

---

2. Kenneth Wuest, *The New Testament: An Expanded Translation* (repr., Grand Rapids, MI: Eerdmans, 1994).

Yes, in this world that moment of elation, of fulfillment, of satisfaction will pass and the clock will begin ticking on the thing itself, but I think God gives us little glimpses of what the true nature of ultimate reality is like, and I think this brief feeling is one of those glimpses. This is what God means when God speaks of making all things new. A new kind of new.

God, help me, even fleetingly, to expand my imagination so that I may experience what you mean when you say, "Behold, I make all things new." Amen.

I Wonder

> *I wonder . . .*
> —*Ray Ashford,* And We Fly Away

Growing up, I had a box full of sleek Hot Wheels and yards and yards of the bright orange tracks along which the little cars zoomed. The loop-the-loop add-on never worked that well, but it did enhance the drama of the crashes. As marshal-general of multiple units of little green plastic soldiers, I strategized over many a pitched battle on the floor of our living room. And I loved my G.I. Joe's—especially the astronaut one. With a flashlight in my right hand and his silver space capsule in my left, he made many a distant journey to imagined worlds where he'd often, in a closet simulating the darkness of outer space, encounter aliens in the form of my sisters' stuffed animals or our family's dachshund, Nietzel. As I got a little older, my brother and I developed whole rosters of fictitious baseball and football teams. We created colorful trading cards with made-up names and detailed stats. Then he would play as one team and I would play as another in our backyard. We'd even get our mother to sing the National Anthem before the momentous first pitch or the opening kickoff of our games. I had a pretty wondrous childhood, and as a kid I had an active imagination.

Our capacity to wonder, to imagine, to play make-believe helps us as we grow up. It improves our brain function. It stimulates creativity. It helps us socialize. It refreshes our stores of energy, calms our anxieties, and nurses our sense of well-being. And while it is commonly said that we tend to lose our sense of wonder as we age, I don't think that is the case. Perhaps we lose our sense of *childlike* wonder, but most of us maintain robust imaginations into our adulthoods; we just utilize them differently as we get older. We enjoy following TV shows that require a complete suspension of disbelief. We rush to movies featuring all manner of superheroes. Some of us dress up and go to the Renaissance Festival or take on the role of an owner in a fantasy football league each fall. We sink ourselves into imagined stories all the time, and it still has the effect of expanding our minds, reenergizing our souls, calming our anxieties, and nurturing along our sense of well-being. Perhaps most importantly, our imaginations help us navigate the terrain of adulthood as we face more and more of life's arduous trials.

The expansive and winsome imagination of a thoughtful Christian writer named Ray Ashford is put to such use in his graceful little book titled *And We Fly Away: Living beyond Alzheimer's*.[1] In spare and poetic prose, Ashford chronicles his wife's descent into dementia, shepherding himself through the exquisitely dark season of loss and grief by the beautiful light of the words "I wonder . . . ." For instance, he explores with penetrating curiosity the question of where the lost part of his wife has gone. Has it been obliterated? Has it just disappeared? Fortified with hope and allied with his faith, he concludes that his God would not permit this and then wonders if a human soul might instead be divisible. He wonders if a soul might be somehow sundered for a time only to be magnificently and eternally made whole again one day. "Could it be, I wonder, that the part of my beloved that has gone, has merely *gone on ahead*, and, there, in that eternal dimension, is awaiting the remnants I can still see, awaiting that triumphant day when once more she will be whole, entire, complete."[2]

I read this passage years ago when my parents were suffering like Ashford's wife and found it comforting. Not necessarily because I thought it was true, but maybe because it just might be. Because it

---

1. Ray Ashford, *And We Fly Away: Living beyond Alzheimer's* (Minneapolis: Fortress Press, 2003).

2. Ibid.

could be. Because it was so lovely. It made me wonder, and the act of wondering somehow offered a measure of healing to my soul.

I don't know, but I wonder . . . if you're facing the unknown, if you're mired in a place of suffering, if you're just stuck, maybe setting aside some time and space to wonder might help. Make a distant journey to an imagined land and explore it. Just because you've left stuffed animals and G.I. Joe's behind doesn't mean this is off-limits. It's not against the rules of adulthood to use the powers of your mind and heart to refresh your energy, calm your anxieties, and nurse your sense of well-being. Swing a flashlight around in the dark and into the realm of the just-might-be.

God, I wonder . . . . Amen.

Love Songs

My name is Nick Cave and I have a few things to tell you.
  —*Nick Cave,* The Secret Life of the Love Song

Do you have a favorite love song? A top three or four? Here are some of mine: "Something" (The Beatles), "God Only Knows" (The Beach Boys), "Every Little Thing She Does Is Magic" (The Police), "Tupelo Honey" (Van Morrison). There are many others, but what's hard to miss whether you're listening to Percy Sledge or Hank Williams, Etta James or Taylor Swift, the Beatles or the Beach Boys, is that the best ones tend to embody both the joy we associate with love *and* the yearning pain we connect with it.

Nick Cave is an Australian singer, songwriter, poet, and author. He lost his father when he was just nineteen in a car accident, and this trauma magnetized him to songwriting. "The way I learned to fill that hole, that void was to write. It provided me," Cave said, "direct access to my imagination, to inspiration, and ultimately, to God."[1] About three years after losing his dad, Cave moved to London and became a part of the emergence of the Gothic Rock movement. As you might imagine from the name, it's dark. The band he started—Nick Cave and the Bad Seeds—continued to develop, drawing inspiration

---

1. Nick Cave, *The Secret Life of the Love Song & The Flesh Made Word: Two Lectures by Nick Cave*, Audio CD, Mute U.S., December 7, 2006. See the two lectures at www.youtube.com/watch?v=uFPicKwiybE and the transcript at everything2.com/title/Nick+Cave%2527s+Love+Song+Lecture.

from Southern spirituals, the blues, and the Old Testament. While his music has always retained a fascination with darkness and death, as he moved more deeply into his career, themes of grace and hints of mercy began to emerge in his compositions as his faith evolved and he pushed the boundaries of his craft as a songwriter. "The actualizing of God through the medium of the love song," he has said, "remains my prime motivation as an artist."[2]

By 1998, Cave was widely regarded as one of the music world's most creative lyricists and was asked to speak at the Vienna Poetry Academy, where he gave a speech titled *The Secret Life of the Love Song*.[3] The speech was so well received that the following year he was asked to give it again in London, during which he said this:

> . . . the Love Song comes in many guises . . . [but] they all address God . . . it's the howl in the void for love and for comfort . . . it's in the cry of one chained to the earth and craving flight . . . the desire to be transported from darkness into light, to be touched by the hand of that which is not of this world. The Love Song is the light of God, deep down, blasting up through our wounds.[4]

That our best love songs tend to blend joy with longing reflects C. S. Lewis's observation that what is most beautiful and sublime in our world always seems to carry a touch of melancholy, a hint of sadness.[5] Lewis posits that this is because even the best earthly pleasures, like our love for each other, is merely a "copy, or echo, or mirage" of the real thing[6]—God's divine love for us and ours for God when we reach our "true country," that more real-than-real eternal realm for which we were created.[7] Reiterating a form of Lewis's idea in his speech, Cave said, "Ultimately, the Love Song

---

2. Ibid.

3. Ibid.

4. Ibid.

5. C. S. Lewis, *The Weight of Glory* (San Francisco: HarperOne, 2001).

6. Ibid.

7. C. S. Lewis, *Mere Christianity* (London: MacMillan Publishing Company, 1984).

exists to fill, with language, the silence between ourselves and God, to decrease the distance between the temporal and the divine."[8]

While in each successive period of his career, Nick Cave has in some sense distanced himself artistically from the world of rock and roll, he has continued to mine its countercultural DNA, coming closer and closer to creating what might be considered a new genre of music that combines all his influences. In his latest album titled *Seven Psalms*,[9] there is love, arresting beauty, longing, faith, and suffering (Cave has tragically lost two of his sons in the last seven years), but at root there is an acknowledgment of the true country of which Lewis spoke.

The cover art for *Seven Psalms* is Bible-black, the title printed soberly in gold, a cross above the artist's name at the bottom in small letters. It was published with these words from Cave: "The seven psalms are presented as one long meditation—on faith, rage, love, grief, mercy, sex, and praise. A veiled, contemplative offering borne of an uncertain time. I hope you like it."[10]

I do. Ambient. Cave's remarkable voice. Beautiful, spoken lyrics from a modern psalmist. It probably won't break into your list of favorite love songs, but maybe a new list is in order: *Love Songs for the True Country*.

> God, "One bright day I will come and I will kneel within your boundless majesty so clear."[11] Amen.

---

8. Cave, *Two Lectures*, CD.
9. Nick Cave and the Bad Seeds, *Seven Psalms*, Goliath Ent, April 28, 2022.
10. Ibid.
11. Ibid., song, "How Long Have I Waited."

Saturday

Community

Then God said: "Let us make mankind in our image, in our likeness . . . ." God saw that all that he made, and it was very good. And there was evening, and there was morning—the sixth day. (Genesis 1:26, 31)

51

Carry Each Other

We get to carry each other . . .

—*U2, "One"*

Director Davis Guggenheim's 2011 documentary film *From the Sky Down* looks back to 1990 and the making of *Achtung Baby*, the seventh studio album of the Irish rock band U2.[1] To set the stage a little, after their success in the 1980s, the group wanted to reinvent themselves in the new decade but struggled to find direction. Seeking to capture some new dynamic energy, they traveled to Hansa Studios in West Berlin just 150 meters from where the Berlin Wall had fallen only months before in 1989. Berlin, perhaps in its own in-between space that winter, proved only cold and bleak, and the band's troubles continued.

The group's lead singer—the person the world knows as Bono—framed their faltering reinvention efforts like this: "You have to reject one expression of the band to get to the next, and in between you have nothing." So, in this vulnerable, uncertain, liminal place, the Hansa sessions were proving volatile, fraught with conflict over whether the band could or even should go on. Floundering personally, relationally, and creatively after more than a decade together,

---

1. *From the Sky Down*, directed by Davis Guggenheim, produced by Ted Skillman, Belisa Balaban, Davis Guggenheim, Brian Celler, and Documentary Partners, September 8, 2011, Toronto International Film Festival, October 29, 2011 (US). All information and quotes concerning U2 in this chapter are from this documentary.

the band members were drifting apart and a breakup seemed almost inevitable. "It wasn't us against them," Bono said. "It was more each one for himself—which betrays the whole concept of a band." U2's guitarist Dave Evans, nicknamed "Edge," recalled, "Everyone began to walk differently, converse differently, carry their cup of tea differently—we all sensed the tension, the doubt; each of us were kind of retreating."

Laboring through a song called "Sick Puppy," which was perhaps a little too on the nose for where they were, they continued to stumble along until something shifted subtly. As they worked, "Sick Puppy" began to morph into a new, far more vigorous tune called "Mysterious Ways" that concerned the mystical work of the Holy Spirit. While Edge was roughing out a bridge from one part of the piece to next, the band's longtime producer Daniel Lanois heard something distinctive in one of the chord progressions that intrigued him. He asked Edge to combine it with another little riff that had arisen as "Mysterious Ways" was trying to take wing.

Lanois quickly moved the band into what they called the big room at Hansa, a larger studio, to see if a new song might materialize. Edge began to fold the two progressions together into one. Bono followed along, beginning to sing not lyrics but in what his bandmates call "Bono-ese"—mumbled notes and vocalizations, experimenting with emotional words, humming along at times within the rudiments of the emergent song.

Then, at one point on the engineer's raw tapes, Bono is heard saying, "Give me an acoustic guitar at the speed of light." With the instrument in his hands, his strumming adding another layer to what was coming together, he continued to sing. "He was calling out chords," U2's bass player Adam Clayton remembered, "trying to figure out where the fertile ground was melodically for him." Lanois recalled the experience as well. "When you're in that moment of inception, there's a momentum that takes you to another place."

They'd come to Berlin hoping for some magic, and now it was happening. And though what was being expressed in this new song was sonically bittersweet, still "there was something eternal, 'upful,' joyful in the melody," Adam said. It was all organic to the struggle yet transcended it. "Nothing was going right and we were suddenly presented with this gift that just kind of arrived," Edge said. The name of Guggenheim's documentary speaks to this phenomenon—something that can't be orchestrated or quite grasped but responds to our exertions, descending from the sky, from heaven to earth, from God to us.

U2 went on to finish their album, which Rolling Stone recently placed at #124 on its list of the 500 greatest albums of all time.[2] (I'd personally rate it higher, but people say I'm a little biased.) The song created in that session in Berlin is called "One." It's sometimes played at weddings, though it's more of a breakup song than a romantic one. More precisely, it's about surviving. And it ends with a solution on the matter: "We get to carry each other. Carry each other."[3]

When you're struggling, when things are bleak, when you're in the midst of a season of dread and dryness, a place of bitter cold—tense, filled with doubt, in retreat—look, listen, even stare into the abyss. Breathe, attuned to the subtleties inside the darkness, inside the silences. Something will emerge with your exertions. Something will descend. Until it does, stay with your bandmates—family, friends, church, community.

We get to carry each other.

God, help us carry each other. Amen.

---

2. Ibid.
3. U2, "One," *Achtung Baby*, Island, 1991.

Failures of Kindness

What I regret most in my life are failures of kindness.
—George Saunders

Joel Lovell of the *New York Times Magazine* wrote the following words concerning the nearly singular gifts of his friend George Saunders and Saunders's short story collections *CivilWarLand in Bad Decline* and *Tenth of December*:

> . . . you read them and you feel known, if that makes any sense. Or, possibly even woollier, you feel as if he understands humanity in a way that no one else quite does, and you're comforted by it. Even if that comfort often comes in very strange packages . . . .[1]

Saunders breaks a lot of stereotypes with both his writing and his approach to life. The trope of the great writer as *tortured soul*, reclusive or volatile, doesn't fit Saunders at all. He seems the opposite—genial and generous. He describes himself as having "a mawkish, natural enthusiasm for things. I like being alive," he says, "in a way that's a little bit cheerleader-ish."[2] His 2021 book, *A Swim in a Pond in the Rain*, is—as far as I can tell halfway through—a four-hundred-page

---

1. Joel Lovell, "George Saunders Has Written the Best Book You'll Read This Year," *New York Times Magazine*, January 3, 2013, www.nytimes.com/2013/01/06/magazine/george-saunders-just-wrote-the-best-book-youll-read-this-year.html.
2. Ibid.

revelation of the creative-writing craft secrets of a generationally talented writer.³ Intricate yet accessible, it's a delightful compilation of the things he teaches aspiring writers each semester at Syracuse University, all delivered with enormous warmth and modesty. Saunders's own mentor, National Medal of the Arts winner and short story writer Tobias Wolff, said of his former student, "George is such a generous spirit, you'd be embarrassed to behave in a small way around him."⁴

While there are dozens of commendable college commencement speeches making the rounds on the internet, Saunders's convocation remarks at Syracuse from almost a decade ago stand out as truly exceptional. And because what I'd like to try to convey can't be done in any better way than to quote Saunders directly, I'm obliged to do so here at length on the subject on which he spoke—our failures of kindness:

> In seventh grade, this new kid joined our class. In the interest of confidentiality, her convocation speech name will be "Ellen." Ellen was small, shy. She wore these blue cat's-eye glasses that, at the time, only old ladies wore. When nervous, which was pretty much always, she had a habit of taking a strand of hair into her mouth and chewing on it.
>
> So, she came to our school and our neighborhood, and was mostly ignored, occasionally teased. I could see this hurt her. I still remember the way she'd look after such an insult: eyes cast down, a little gut-kicked, as if, having just been reminded of her place in things, she was trying, as much as possible, to disappear. After a while she'd drift away, hair strand still in her mouth. At home, I imagined, after school, her mother would say: *"How was your day, sweetie?"* and she'd say, *"Oh, fine."* And her mother would say, *"Making any friends?"* and she'd go, *"Sure, lots."* Sometimes I'd see her hanging around alone in her front yard, as if afraid to leave it.
>
> And then—they moved. That was it. No tragedy, no big final hazing. One day she was there, next day she wasn't. End of

---

3. George Saunders, *A Swim in the Pond in the Rain* (New York: Random House, 2021).

4. Lovell, "George Saunders Has Written the Best Book."

story . . . . Why, forty-two years later, am I still thinking about it? Relative to most of the other kids, I was actually pretty nice to her. I never said an unkind word to her. In fact, I sometimes even (mildly) defended her. But still. It bothers me. So, here's something I know to be true, although it's a little corny, and I don't quite know what to do with it: What I regret most in my life are failures of kindness. Those moments when another human being was there, in front of me, suffering, and I responded . . . sensibly. Reservedly. Mildly.[5]

I have my own regrets about failures of kindness I've perpetrated against the unsuspecting and undeserving. I wince at myself, feeling the force of my negligence viscerally. As I get older, I see such unforced errors even more starkly—the smallness, the thoughtlessness, the acute failures in courage, the fundamental misunderstanding about what is most important, eternally important. And perhaps worst of all, when I look back over space and time between now and seventh grade, or to such regretful moments in adulthood, or even to last week, really all there is to do is feel the pain that was inflicted and say it won't happen again.

To now refrain from such harm.

And to err on the side of kindness.

In kindness, God, may I not be sensible, reserved, or mild but, today, this week, and forever more, positively alive with it. Amen.

---

5. Rob Enslin, "Professor and Author George Saunders's 2013 Convocation Address: English professor, renowned author tells undergraduates to 'err in the direction of kindness,'" *Syracuse University*, originally posted May 20, 2013, and updated May 5, 2021, artsandsciences.syracuse.edu/news-all/news-2013/2013-george_saunders_convocation/.

The Dances You've Already Had

No matter what, nobody can take away the dances you've already had.
—*Gabriel García Márquez*

Gabriel García Márquez was a Columbian writer. He remains best known for his epic 1967 novel, *One Hundred Years of Solitude*, a fantastical story concerning seven generations of a single family living in the fictitious South American town of Macondo.[1] Márquez plumbs themes related to fortune and misfortune and how they mix together, leaving the reader to conclude that human nature has a way of ensuring that history repeats itself.

When asked if he'd like to win the Nobel Prize in Literature someday, Márquez quipped, "I would certainly be interested in deserving it."[2] He eventually won the award in 1982, the Nobel Committee extending the honor to him "for his novels and short stories in which the fantastic and the realistic are combined . . . ."[3]

---

1. Gabriel García Márquez, *One Hundred Years of Solitude* (repr., New York: Harper Perennial Modern Classics, 2006).
2. Gabriel García Márquez, "The Art of Fiction No. 69," interview by Peter H. Stone, *The Paris Review* 82 (Winter 1981), available at *AZ Quotes*, www.azquotes.com/quote/1273400.
3. "The Nobel Prize in Literature 1982: Gabriel García Márquez," *The Nobel Prize: Nobel Prize Outreach AB 2023*, September 21, 2023, www.nobelprize.org/

These were apt words, as Márquez was the chief progenitor of the literary style now known as "magical realism" in which a writer places the supernatural, the whimsical, and the unbelievable in the mundane context of an everyday setting. Márquez said his style developed as he remembered the way his maternal grandmother used to tell him stories when he was a boy. She would drop extraordinary events, people, and things into her tales "as if they were simply an aspect of everyday life," he recalled. "What was most important," he added, "was the expression on her face. No matter how supernatural and fantastic the event, she told them with complete naturalness . . . not chang[ing] her expression at all."[4] His novels, he acknowledged, only came together when he began to write and communicate them with "the same expression with which my grandmother told them."[5]

With this approach, Márquez began to create characters who were, for instance, constantly followed around by bright yellow butterflies—a symbol of love and infinite hope. He created scenes like the one in *One Hundred Years of Solitude* in which a woman named Remedios the Beauty ascends into the heavens on a windy day having been caught up in a sheet she was pinning to a clothesline. In Márquez's final novel, he wistfully penned a memorable line that captures, in a sense, another way of grasping the idea of magical realism: "No matter what," he wrote, "nobody can take away the dances you've already had."[6]

The origin of dancing remains a mystery, but it's undeniably universal. It must bestow some sort of evolutionary advantage on us as we've been dancing quite a while, and we whose genes have

---

prizes/literature/1982/summary/.

4. Dasso Saldívar, *García Márquez: El viaje a la semilla: la biografía* (Madrid: Alfaguara, 1997).

5. Anahi Rami, "Nobel winner Garcia Marquez, master of magical realism, dies at 87," *Reuters*, April 17, 2014, www.reuters.com/article/us-garciamarquez/nobel-winner-garcia-marquez-master-of-magical-realism-dies-at-87-idIN-BREA3F1LY20140417.

6. Carl Fussman, "Gabriel Garcia Marquez: What I've Learned," *Esquire Magazine*, April 18, 2014, www.esquire.com/entertainment/books/a28460/what-ive-learned-gabriel-garcia-marquez/.

so stoutly persisted in this world are still doing it today. The oldest cave painting that likely represents human dancing appears to have been created some 9,000 years ago.[7] Dancing seems to be deeply programmed into our wiring; research has shown that infants as young as three months of age respond to musical pulses with spontaneous limb movements.[8] Dancing floods our systems with happy chemicals like dopamine and endorphins.[9] Dancing has been shown to reduce the risk of dementia in the elderly.[10] Psychologically, it enables us to self-induce the soothing effect of being rocked like we were as babies. Physiologically, we know modern health clubs typically offer a variety of classes combining music and different forms of dancing because it reduces the perception of exertion as we exercise.

If we open our imaginations, the fantastic and the real combine rather magically in the human experience of dancing. Pair this notion with the concept of memory, and we see its potency even more clearly. Think about it. It's not hard for most of us to reach back into our minds to a magical but real moment in our past that involved a beautiful dance in community with others: a middle school crush, a high school prom, a college party, a wedding reception, an amazing concert, an anniversary date, or maybe just a little celebratory jig in your living room when your team won or in the backyard, one hand in the air, when something turned out especially well.

The phenomenon of what happens when we dance and how we're able to miraculously access and bring forth the most beautiful

---

7. See "History of Dance," *Dance Facts*, www.dancefacts.net/dance-history/history-of-dance/.

8. Shinya Fujii, Hama Watanabe, Hiroki Oohashi et al., "Precursors of Dancing and Singing to Music in Three- to Four-Months-Old Infants," *Plos One*, May 16, 2014, doi.org/10.1371/journal.pone.0097680.

9. Hannah John, "British Science Festival: 7 ways dancing can improve your life," *British Science Association*, September 25, 2019, www.britishscienceassociation.org/blogs/bsa-blog/7-ways-dancing-can-improve-your-life.

10. "Can Dancing Prevent Alzheimer's Disease?" *Bethesda*, June 20, 2022, citing "Leisure Activities and the Risk of Dementia in the Elderly," Joe Verghese, MD, et al., presented in part at the 127th annual meeting of the American Neurological Association, New York, October 12–16, 2002, www.nejm.org/doi/full/10.1056/NEJMoa022252.

memories—the sights, the sounds, the feel—provides persuasive evidence that this world God made is not without its own brand of magic. If you ever feel the shadow of misfortune eclipsing your day, recall the arresting and durable power embedded inside the memory of the dances you've already had. No one can take them away. And since human nature has a history of repeating itself, surely there are more dances ahead.

> *God, thank you for the dances we've already shared and for the ones ahead as well. Amen.*

Mistrust the Rush

And it was so, when Elijah heard it... (1 Kings 19:13)

A few weeks ago, I was speaking to some friends about a controversial topic. As is often the case following such dialogues, the next day I replayed the conversation in my mind, thinking of all sorts of great things I should've said to make my points more emphatic and effective. Had I been able to better marshal my righteous arguments, I thought, that rush of adrenaline, that victorious feeling of forcing my interlocutors into a dramatic surrender, would have been mine.

The problem with this notion is that things don't really work like that. Even if our point of view seems sound and righteous to us, human minds aren't typically changed by pithy "drop-the-mic" declarations, clever social media memes, or even superior arguments. They're changed over time through a series of subtle moments and thoughtful exchanges within our relationships—that is, by evolution. Through an almost imperceptible process, the vision of who we are and how the world works around us is slowly adjusted. I'm reminded of C. S. Lewis's account of how, after years of self-study and conversation with friends on the subject of faith, he realized on one sunny morning in transit to the zoo that he had become a Christian. "When we set out I did not believe that Jesus Christ is the son of God, and when we reached the zoo, I did," Lewis wrote in his book, *Surprised by Joy*.[1]

---

1. C. S. Lewis, *Surprised by Joy* (San Francisco: HarperOne, 2017).

Although God has famously given us a series of commandments to follow, there's good evidence that God is aware that the human mind is often more readily nudged than commanded. The encounter the prophet Elijah had with God bears this out:

> And, behold, the LORD passed by, and a great and strong wind rent the mountains, and broke in pieces the rocks before the LORD, but the LORD was not in the wind; and after the wind an earthquake, but the LORD was not in the earthquake; and after the earthquake a fire, but the LORD was not in the fire; and after the fire a still small voice. And it was so, when Elijah heard it . . . . (1 Kings 19:11-13, KJV)

A study of this passage's context reveals that, out of a well-founded fear for his life, Elijah really didn't want to get back into the "prophet-to-Israel business," but God changed his mind through a quiet voice that seems to equate closely with Elijah's own conscience. Listening to this inner dialogue, not the blustery wind or the shaking of the earth or the dramatic fire, is what changed Elijah's mind, suggesting that our miraculous capacity to talk through things internally evolves our thinking and has the power to redirect our moral vision. This compelling narrative also raises one more crucial point: the quiet voice of conscience—the one we should always listen for—often speaks to us in inconvenient ways.

In her collection of soulful essays titled *When I Was a Child I Read Books*, Pulitzer Prize–winning novelist Marilynne Robinson laments, "The language of public life has lost the character of generosity."[2] While Robinson's essays give us some direction for how to recover this virtue, my recent interaction with friends has directed me to my own. The first step, I think, is to mistrust the rush we feel when forcefully arguing for what we think is a righteous cause. Perhaps we ought to question ourselves most when we receive the boost of adrenaline we associate with putting someone else in their place. That's not the voice of God. It's much likelier that when God speaks to us and even through us in these situations, it will be accompanied not by an

---

2. Marilynne Robinson, *When I Was a Child I Read Books* (repr., Picador, 2013).

adrenaline rush but by a quiet feeling of inconvenience that urges us to treat one another with an extra measure of grace, an open mind, and a deeper sense of generosity.

Rather than wishing I had capped off the evening with my friends with a windy, emotionally satisfying, earth-shaking, firestorm mic-drop of a moment in which I magically commandeered their moral imaginations from them, I should look for another chance to sit down with them in community, in communion, find my own still small voice, and hope I encounter theirs.

God, help me to hear and listen to your inconvenient voice as I encounter others. Amen.

# Tribe

> *Genetic adaptations take around 25,000 years to appear in humans, so the enormous changes that came ... in the last 10,000 years have hardly begun to affect our gene pool.*
>
> —*Sebastian Junger,* Tribe

Sebastian Junger seems afraid of very little. With a degree in cultural anthropology, he embarked on a career as a freelance writer researching a series of hazardous subjects. In a participatory way that routinely risked both life and limb, Junger studied and then wrote about some of the most dangerous things human beings can do. His first book, *The Perfect Storm*, is a riveting account about the perils of the Atlantic commercial fishing industry that led many to hail Junger as a new Ernest Hemingway.[1]

In 2000, Junger traveled to Afghanistan to profile Northern Alliance leader Ahmed Shah Massoud, who was later assassinated by the Taliban just hours before the World Trade Center and Pentagon were attacked on September 11, 2001. Then, when American troops went into Afghanistan, Junger embedded himself in the 173rd Airborne. *Restrepo*, his documentary about the platoon he was with, was nominated for an Academy Award.[2] He has come so close to the fighting

---

1. Sebastian Junger, *Tribe: On Homecoming and Belonging* (New York: Simon and Schuster, 2016).
2. Ibid.

that he was diagnosed with and continues to suffer episodically from post-traumatic stress disorder. His book *Fire* and another titled *War* recount his time in Afghanistan, and his book *Tribe*, published in 2016, details his experience of returning home to the United States from these war zones.[3]

While *Tribe* touches on Junger's PTSD, the book focuses on how human beings have evolved. Our ancestors who thrived and therefore survived, he writes, were part of small nomadic communities—groups of about forty to fifty people who lived with one another in deeply linked, interconnected ways.[4] However, as the agricultural age, then the industrial age, and now our own technological age arrived, Junger suggests that we've become more and more removed from how we are evolutionarily designed to flourish. While genetically, biologically, we're not that different from our distant ancestors who were evolutionarily programmed to thrive in small, tightly bound groups, we now live in a whole new environment. "Genetic adaptations," Junger writes, "take around 25,000 years to appear in humans, so the enormous changes that came . . . in the last 10,000 years have hardly begun to affect our gene pool."[5] The world has changed so much, he says, that for the first time in all of human history, a person might go an entire day, a whole season, or even most of an entire lifetime interacting not with family or tribe but exclusively with strangers. One could say that this is not how we're supposed to live, but it would be more accurate to say this is not how we're designed to thrive.

Again, Sebastian Junger seems afraid of very little, but what seems to scare him most is the threat that we are all being captured within this paradox of modern life. While in many ways we are more connected than ever, we still feel deeply, desperately, and dangerously alone. Our biology tells us we're a curious batch of wandering creatures who flourish most when we are both proximally and emotionally linked in close community with a contingent of around forty to fifty people, but our new way of life, conducted mostly in

---

3. Ibid.
4. Ibid.
5. Ibid.

urbanized modern settings, has begun to conspire against us. We've become frenetic yet sedentary, weary yet sleep-deprived, overfed yet malnourished, wealthy yet bereft. Though we're *technologically* intertwined with one another, *physically* we're more socially isolated than ever. Junger's conclusion is that our modern ways and means of living have torn the social fabric that has always characterized the human experience, offering back something terribly brutalizing to the human spirit.

So, what do we do about it?

The name our church has given collectively to our fifth through seventh graders is "The Tribe." Currently, there are about forty to fifty in this little community. They have their own dedicated space. Though it's not outside, it is filled with light and is their own. It's designed with places for vibrant social connection and safe spots for the kids to think and brood if they want to. Each week, the Tribers take up the wisdom of ancient stories found in Scripture to further connect with one another and to link themselves more transcendently with the wisdom of past generations. The language of their liturgy and their leadership speaks poignantly time and time again about the central idea of being together, that is, of *belonging* not only to God but also to one another. The Tribe seems to be thriving.

How do we push back against the headwinds of our environment and age that Sebastian Junger writes about? I'm not completely sure, but this seems to be a good place to start.

God, in places of fear, in places of anxiety, may we find belonging. Amen.

Getting Home

To be happy at home is . . . the end to which every enterprise and labor tends . . . .
—*Dr. Samuel Johnson*

Not long ago, I found myself sleeping all night on a metal bench in an airport, forsaken by all but the graveyard shift and a handful of other weary travelers at the usually bustling terminal. When a TSA employee roused me from my fitful slumber at 5 a.m. and told me to move along, I obediently arose, my contacts sticking to my eyes, the strap of my cumbersome carry-on bag cutting into my shoulder blade, and stumbled toward the glowing blue light of the arrival/departure board. My flight remained delayed. I still had no idea when I might get home.

Songwriters know it. *Home* is a lyrical word that evokes deep feelings. Scores of songs invoke the idea, all penned to pluck the listener's heartstrings, reminding them of where they were before and want to be again. "Take Me Home Country Roads," "California Dreamin'," "Homeward Bound," "Can't Find My Way Home," "Sweet Home Alabama"—these songs bring to mind a pining feeling, a yearning to get back home again.

Moviemakers know it too. *The Wizard of Oz*; *The Trip to Bountiful*; *Planes, Trains, and Automobiles*; *Toy Story*; and *The Martian* are all films that follow compelling characters on compelling journeys trying to get home against the odds. We identify with their plight because we're well-acquainted with the pain of dislocation and the desire to return to the place where our heart belongs.

And creative writers and storytellers know the mesmerizing, magnetic power of home too. The primal urge to get home is the animating force behind the most famous tale in the history of our species—Homer's *Odyssey*—likely written in the seventh century BC after being passed down through word of mouth for who knows how long. How revealing is it that the prototype adventure story of our species—the one that tells us so much about our nature, our aspirations, and our failings, takes as its main concern a hero's struggle to return home? Odysseus may be seeking glory. He may be pursuing the favor of the gods along the way. But more than anything else, the guy just wants to get back to his wife, his son, and his dog.

Eighteenth-century English poet, playwright, and dictionary-maker Dr. Samuel Johnson asserted, "To be happy at home is the ultimate result of all ambition, the end to which every enterprise and labor tends, and of which every desire prompts the prosecution."[1] I think he may be on to something. While this is a generalization, if you consider why human beings think ahead, plan, and strategize about the future, why we toil and labor, and why we're so rambunctiously inclined toward conflict and combat, you'll find that we're all just trying to secure, maintain, and enjoy a safe place where we can be ourselves, be with family, live, grow, flourish, raise our children and then launch them out into the world so they can do the same.

It's interesting that Jesus so swiftly reaches for the metaphor of home when he describes eternity, the idea of heaven, to his disciples. There is something especially comforting about the words he chooses: "Let not your heart be troubled," he said. "In my Father's house are many mansions" (John 14:1, 2, KJV).

When you find yourself at home with the people you associate with home, look around, and for a brief moment realize that you're experiencing the feeling songwriters, filmmakers, and generations of storytellers often try to evoke—the one that those away from home yearn to feel. Grasp the notion that you have the thing they describe

---

1. Samuel Johnson, *Rambler* #68, November 10, 1750, www.samueljohnson.com/happines.html.

as most desirable. The thing folks marooned in airports crave. In this moment, it's yours. Extract its strength and its blessing. Fully understand that this moment is the one you've industriously pursued with both great consideration and strain. This is it. It's a hint of eternity, in a small dose, offered to you to experience *right now*.

If you're far from the place you call home, either due to distance or because you're in a circumstance that is far from the ideal of home you've imagined for yourself, know that the profound exchange Jesus had with his followers is evidence that God knows what you yearn for and has given reliable assurance that the story ends with what you've been missing—the joy of truly getting home.

God, help me get home. Amen.

Eleanor Rigby

Eleanor Rigby picks up the rice in the church where a wedding has been.... All the lonely people, Where do they all come from? All the lonely people, Where do they all belong?
—*Paul McCartney, "Eleanor Rigby"*

Robert Putnam is a smart social scientist. More than two decades ago, in his book *Bowling Alone*, Putnam asserted that we as a society have grown ever more disconnected from each other. In his writing, he popularized the term and notion of "social capital"—that is, our stock, our reserves, our network of connections with colleagues, friends, and even casual acquaintances that provide us with the sense of security, belonging, meaning, hope, and happiness we all need in our lives.[1] Social capital helps us avert the sort of despair the Beatles sang about in their poignant 1966 song "Eleanor Rigby."

Putnam's exhaustive research, interviews, and data show us that we now belong to fewer organizations, reach out to our neighbors less, meet with friends less, and socialize with our families less than we used to. We are even bowling alone—hence the title of his book.

*Father McKenzie, writing the words of a sermon
that no one will hear, no one comes near . . .*

---

1. Robert Putnam, *Bowling Alone: The Collapse and Revival of American Community* (New York: Touchstone Books by Simon & Schuster, 2001).

All the lonely people, Where do they all come from?
All the lonely people, Where do they all belong?[2]

Edmund Burke was an Irish-born statesman, economist, and philosopher who served in the British House of Commons between 1766 and 1794. He wrote and spoke prolifically on the development of human virtue, stability in a culture, and how to establish a government that might redound to the benefit of all its people. Most interestingly, he insisted that the effort in these realms must start on a small scale from the bottom up.

> To love the *little platoon* we belong to in society is the first principle—the first link—in the series by which we proceed toward a love of mankind. Those without a little platoon are going to suffer from a diminished love of mankind, and those places where the platoon is absent are going to be places of anxiety.[3]

"For two years" John Leland of the *New York Times* wrote as he reflected on the Covid-19 pandemic, "you didn't see friends like you used to. You missed your colleagues from work, even the barista on the way there. You were lonely. We all were."[4] Leland's article then describes what neuroscientists tell us happened to our brains during the first two years of the pandemic. Was it bad? Well, it wasn't good.

By now, probably no one needs to tell you that being isolated increases your risk of depression, anxiety, and addiction. No one needs to remind you that researchers at Brigham Young found that the psychological effects of loneliness correlate closely with the physical effect of smoking fifteen cigarettes a day.[5] Or that weak social networks reduce your immune response, putting you at a higher risk

---

2. John Lennon and Paul McCartney, "Eleanor Rigby," *Revolver*, Parlophone (UK), Capitol (US), 1966.

3. Edmund Burke, *Reflections on the Revolution in France* (London: 1867).

4. John Leland, "How Loneliness Is Damaging Our Health," *New York Times*, April 20, 2022, www.nytimes.com/2022/04/20/nyregion/loneliness-epidemic.html.

5. Ibid.

of heart disease, cancer, stroke, hypertension, and dementia. We've all heard and read this by now. We just need to know how to fix it.

Consider everything bigger than your family but smaller than the government—*what are you a part of?* The number of community institutions you're connected to goes a long way in predicting your well-being. Consider not diminishing but increasing your involvement in the community, the institution, the group, whatever it is, that delivers the most meaning to you. Lean into that one—whatever it might be. But do consider this quick public service announcement as well:

- Regular participation in a religious community is clearly linked with higher levels of happiness.[6]
- Even if one holds little stake in the sacraments and sermons, social science research indicates the resilience benefits accrue from simply being an active part of a congregation regardless of one's lack of, or struggles with faith itself.[7]
- Healthy marriages and religious attendance are closely correlated with each other, and church-going kids have measurably better relationships with their parents, other adults, and their peers.[8]
- For someone at the median national income of $56,500, spending two or more hours devoted to religious activity in a given week is associated with more happiness than getting a $20,000 raise.[9]

It is interesting that Lennon and McCartney set their lament about loneliness largely in an empty church. If church was a drug, our

---

6. "Religion's Relationship to Happiness," *Civic Engagement and Health around the World*, Pew Research Center, January 31, 2019, www.pewresearch.org/religion/2019/01/31/religions-relationship-to-happiness-civic-engagement-and-health-around-the-world/.
7. Tim Carney, *Alienated America: Why Some Places Thrive While Others Collapse*, illus. ed. (New York: Harper, 2019).
8. Robert Putnam, *Our Kids* (repr., New York: Simon & Schuster, 2016).
9. Robert Putnam and David Campbell, *American Grace: How Religion Divides and Unites Us* (New York: Simon & Schuster, 2012).

doctors would be prescribing it for our loneliness. They might even put it in the water.

All the lonely people, where do they belong?

God, help me see the value of embedding myself into a community. Amen.

The Fire

The object of hope is a future good—difficult but possible to obtain.

—Thomas Aquinas

In her collection of essays titled *On Reading Well: Finding the Good Life through Great Books*, Karen Swallow Prior takes her readers on a guided tour through several great works of literature that shine a spotlight on human virtue—the cardinal virtues like Justice and Courage; the theological virtues like Faith, Hope, and Love; and the heavenly virtues like Patience, Kindness, and Humility.[1]

In each chapter, Prior selects a classic book by a famous or highly regarded author who transmits a deep and clarifying knowledge of one of these virtues through fictional narrative, that is, through the art of story. For instance, from Dickens's *A Tale of Two Cities*, we learn of Justice. From Shusako Endo's *Silence*, we examine Faith. From Jane Austen's *Persuasion*, we're guided toward Patience. And from Cormac McCarthy's dark, apocalyptic novel called *The Road*—as unlikely as it might seem—we learn of hope, as McCarthy brilliantly affirms all that we sense is best in our souls despite the bleak, nihilistic world in which his story is set.[2]

---

1. Karen Swallow Prior, *On Reading Well: Finding the Good Life through Great Books*, illus. ed. (Ada, MI: Brazos Press, 2018).
2. Cormac McCarthy, *The Road* (New York: Knopf Doubleday Publishing Group, 2006).

The Road is a simple yet harrowing tale of a nameless father and son, referred to in McCarthy's spare prose only as "the man" and "the boy."[3] As the story unfolds, the man's wife, the boy's mother, is gone, and the two must reckon with the darkest of realities—the challenge of survival amid the aftermath of an existential (though largely unexplained) global cataclysm. Imperiled by unspeakable horrors at every turn, they skillfully avert the harm other survivors wish to inflict on them as they traverse a cold and barren landscape toward the promise of coastal warmth, the sea, and a place where perhaps a reconstituted civilization might exist. As they travel on and off the road, the father shepherds and protects his son while the son, in his innocence and devotion to his father, reminds them both (along with the reader) of what is good and right in what remains of their broken world. McCarthy renders their tender exchanges in spartan dialogue:

> We're going to be okay, aren't we Papa.
> Yes. We are.
> And nothing bad is going to happen to us.
> That's right.
> Because we're carrying the fire.[4]

The father and son refer to "the fire" several times in conversation, though McCarthy never directly tells the reader what is meant by this. It's hardly necessary to know. Whatever the fire is, it's the reason the son refers to his father and to himself as "the good guys." Whatever the fire is, it suggests that even in our darkest hours, transcendence is still offered to us through the selfless love a father has for his child. Whatever the fire is, it captures the indelible notion of hope—the thing that we pray emerges when the urge to give up arises inside of us.

Thankfully, we don't live in a post-apocalyptic world, but I think this metaphor of a fire inside of us may be helpful to think about. Take a close measure of the contours of hope within you right now. What keeps you going through the difficult terrain of life, week after

---

3. Ibid.
4. Ibid.

week and month after month? What tells you that the good you yearn for is not impossible? The "fire" may be hard to define, but it's the thing inside us that pushes back against the nihilism so prevalent in our world today. It's what tells us that transcendence is still available to us through sacrificial love. *This is hope.* In the face of a broken world, there's nothing wrong with acknowledging that it's difficult to have hope sometimes. It takes practice and energy to hope. It also takes skill to avoid the things that divert us from hope.

If you're dispirited or disoriented and looking to find your way back to hope, back to yourself, you'll not find it in dehumanizing anyone—even the ones you consider your enemy—with anger or contempt. It's only with love for one another that we find our way back. Only in practicing the virtue we wish to propagate.

God, help me carry the fire. Amen.

The Effect of Your Being

But the effect of her being on those around her was incalculably diffusive: for the growing good of the world is partly dependent on unhistoric acts; and that things are not so ill with you and me as they might have been is half owing to the number who lived faithfully a hidden life, and rest in unvisited tombs.
—*George Eliot,* Middlemarch

There are some terrific literary entries for best last lines in a book. Here are a few:

- "After all, tomorrow is another day." (*Gone with the Wind*, Margaret Mitchell)[1]
- "It is a far, far better thing that I do, than I have ever done; it is a far, far better rest that I go to than I have ever known." (*A Tale of Two Cities*, Charles Dickens)[2]
- "'God's in his heaven, all's right with the world,' whispered Anne softly." (*Anne of Green Gables*, Lucy Maud Montgomery)[3]
- "But, in spite of these deficiencies, the wishes, the hopes, the confidence, the predictions of the small band of true friends who

---

1. Margaret Mitchell, *Gone with the Wind* (repr., Pocket Books, 2008).
2. Charles Dickens, *A Tale of Two Cities* (repr., Signet, 2007).
3. Lucy Maud Montgomery, *Anne of Green Gables* (repr., Wordsworth Editions, 2018).

witnessed the ceremony, were fully answered in the perfect happiness of the union." (*Emma*, Jane Austen)⁴

Alice Walker's last line of *The Color Purple* is another strong candidate, as is Yann Martel's last sentence from *Life of Pi*. But my vote goes to *Middlemarch*. Mary Ann Evans, writing under the pen name George Eliot, describes at the end of her novel the life of her heroine, Dorothea Brooke:

> But the effect of her being on those around her was incalculably diffusive: for the growing good of the world is partly dependent on unhistoric acts; and that things are not so ill with you and me as they might have been is half owing to the number who lived faithfully a hidden life, and rest in unvisited tombs.⁵

Middlemarch, published in installments in 1871 and 1872, is the story of provincial life in a settled English community facing the threats and possibilities of changing times. Evans/Eliot threads in and out of a series of compelling, intersecting stories and relationships, advancing themes concerning idealism and self-interest, religion and hypocrisy, politics and education, and, perhaps most centrally, the status of women and the nature of marriage. Dorothea, the book's protagonist, is idealistic, kind, intelligent, and full of noble aspiration, but her life, while salutary in most every respect, doesn't play out as she had hoped. This last line leaves the reader not only with beautiful consolation but also with a suspicion that the story in its conclusion has landed on one of life's most resonant and enduring truths.

The movie *A Hidden Life*, written and directed by Terrance Malick, is based on the true but relatively unknown story of Franz Jägerstätter, an Austrian farmer who refused to fight for the Third

---

4. Jane Austen, *Emma* (repr., Penguin Classics, 2003).
5. George Eliot, *Middlemarch: A Study of Provincial Life* (repr., Read & Co. Classics, 2020).

Reich.[6] Drafted to serve, Jägerstätter declines. Despite hostile pressure from neighbors, political and religious leaders in his village, and vindictive German officials, Franz remains steadfast, leaning on his deep faith and the strength of his wife. When offered non-combatant duty if he will only swear an oath to Hitler, he continues to refuse. He is soon shipped away and imprisoned in the harshest of conditions. Beaten and abused, eventually he is put on trial and found guilty of treason. The judge who sentences him to death tells him, "Do you imagine that anything you do will change the course of this war? That anyone outside this court will ever hear of you? No one will be changed. The world will go on as before. You'll vanish." However, when Franz departs the room, the judge—now alone—sits down in the chair Jägerstätter has vacated and gazes down at his hands on his knees as if trying to imagine what it might be like to be such a person. At the conclusion of the film, these words appear:

> . . . for the growing good of the world is partly dependent on unhistoric acts; and that things are not so ill with you and me as they might have been is half owing to the number who lived faithfully a hidden life, and rest in unvisited tombs.

As a minister, I've eulogized some remarkable souls. I can't say that any of them were famous, though a few did quite heroic things. Most of them simply led good lives, contributing incrementally to the growing good of the world. Generous of spirit, they gave without seeking recognition and left things better than they came to them. I'm persuaded that in the end, things are not so ill with you and me today as they might have been is half owing to the faithful, quiet, even hidden lives of such people. I can't recall where all of them now rest, but when I gaze down at my hands on my knees in prayer, I hope to be such a person.

God, may I become a part of the growing good of my community—and the world. Amen.

---

6. *A Hidden Life*, directed by Terrance Malick, produced by Elisabeth Bentley et al., 2019.

I Wish I'd Known That about Him...

In this passage... I think we find the essence of religion.
—George McDonald

After many memorial services, it's not uncommon to hear someone say, "I wish I'd known that about him" or "I can't believe I never heard that about her." In those moments, it strikes me as most regretful that we don't have a practical way to broadcast the unique stories of our lives more effectively to a wider audience—while we're still living.

Our families know our deep biographies. Our close friends are privy to our most compelling experiences. But much of our backstory, the winding paths of our personal journeys, and especially the more granular details of our inner lives seem to remain largely shrouded from our broader circle of friends, colleagues, and acquaintances. Perhaps this is just the nature of things, but it does seem a shame that it's often not until a person is gone that we manage to dedicate some time to piece together their stories—stories from which we gather the true meaning and a fuller understanding of their lives.

I suppose it takes time for the wider spiritual implications of a life come into relief—to see that the pediatrician we know, it turns out, was as much a healer of souls as she was an MD; that the fellow who was always tinkering with machines solved all sorts of problems in the machinery of the lives of others; that the guy down the street who loved to garden as a hobby was also a nurturer of the most fragile among us; that the soldier was a spiritual sentinel, a defender of the noblest ideals in the world; that the woman who everyone knew threw a good party was really an ambassador of Christ's hospitality her whole life.

Scottish author and poet George McDonald was a forerunner and decisive influence on C. S. Lewis, J. R. R. Tolkien, and Madeline L'Engle, as well as Auden, Twain, Chesterton, and many others. Long before these beloved authors came onto the literary scene, McDonald was writing mystical stories and poignant fairy tales as a medium to explore the human condition and the significance of our faith. And as a minister, he was especially good at shedding light on seemingly impenetrable passages of Scripture. For instance, he points an imaginative spotlight on an obscure verse from the book of Revelation and its mysterious reference to an unusual gift God bestows upon those who hold fast to their faith: "Whoever has ears, let them hear what the Spirit says to the churches. To the one who is victorious, I will give . . . that person a *white stone* with a new name written on it, known only to the one who receives it" (Rev 21:7). "In this passage about the gift of the white stone," McDonald wrote, "I think we find the essence of religion."[1]

From this verse, McDonald suggests that God has a true name for each of us. Though it remains unknown to us now, when we receive this stone, the name will express and capture the essence of who we are—"that being, whom He had in his thought when He began to make the child, and whom He kept in his thought through the long process of creation that went to realize the idea."[2] McDonald then concludes with this: "To tell the name is to seal the success—to say, '*In thee I am also well pleased.*'"[3]

What do you think of this? What might be written on your stone? Have you considered what God might be whispering, singing, sighing, laughing, or speaking into creation through your soul? Widen your imagination and give it some thought. Perhaps you're

---

1. George MacDonald, in *George MacDonald: An Anthology (365 Readings)*, ed. C. S. Lewis (Deckle Edge, 2015).

2. MacDonald, *George MacDonald*, 10.

3. Ibid.

not an insurance adjuster but a rescuer of those in crisis. Maybe you're not a geologist but a steward of creation, focused on lifting the poor from poverty. Could it be you're not a teacher but a lantern-bearer lighting a path for the young? Perhaps you're more pilgrim than student. Maybe more spiritual explorer than truck driver.

What is God saying into the world, to your community, to your family through you? What do you aspire to embody? What are you seeking to incarnate? We have all been awarded a useful instrument—a human life with a body, a voice, a vocation, gifts, talents, space, time, and relationships. If you had to boil yourself down to a singular word or idea, what might be written on your stone? Put another way, what do people not know about you that they should? What does God know about you that others should know too?

God, what might be written on my stone? Amen.

Sunday

I've heard a saying among preachers I know regarding the rhythm of their lives. They sometimes refer to "the relentless approach of the Sabbath."

Given all the demands Sunday places on pastors, I can imagine how the responsibility of preparing and presenting a sermon each week might overshadow other things. It must seem that as soon as one service concludes, the next one is upon him, upon her. We should be glad that such demands do not land upon us all.

However, this notion of *the relentless approach of the Sabbath* might be something we should all take to heart in some way. For anyone who takes his or her relationship with God seriously, the Sabbath is supposed to be the most consequential day of the week. We should build our weeks around it. It should, like it does for the preachers among us, occupy considerable space in our minds and exert an influence on our days, a gravity for ordering our weeks. In some significant and meaningful way, our lives should revolve around the Sabbath if we're taking our spiritual health seriously, not to mention our physical and mental health.

In addition to worshiping faithfully in community with one another each week, we should also do as God did on the seventh day and find time and space to *rest*.

As such, there is probably no better way to conclude a book about following the creation narrative as a pattern for our lives than this:

By the seventh day God had finished the work he had been doing; so on the seventh day he rested from all his work. Then God blessed the seventh day and made it holy, because on it he rested from all the work of creating that he had done. (Genesis 2:2-3)

Let us go and do likewise.

www.ingramcontent.com/pod-product-compliance
Lightning Source LLC
Chambersburg PA
CBHW071000160426
43193CB00012B/1857